Lightening the Load

Lightening the Load
Labour-saving technologies and practices
for rural women

Marilyn Carr with Maria Hartl

Published by International Fund for Agricultural Development (IFAD)
and Practical Action Publishing Ltd

Enabling poor rural people
to overcome poverty

Published by International Fund for Agricultural Development (IFAD)
and
Practical Action Publishing Ltd
Schumacher Centre for Technology and Development
Bourton on Dunsmore, Rugby,
Warwickshire, CV23 9QZ, UK
www.practicalactionpublishing.org

ISBN 978 185339 689 2 (Practical Action Publishing)
ISBN 978 92 9072 102 4 (IFAD)

A catalogue record for this book is available from the British Library.

The authors have asserted thier rights under the Copyright Designs and Patents Act
1988 to be identified as authors of this work.

The designations employed and the presentation of material in this publication do
not imply the expression of any opinion whatsoever on the part of the Organisation
and/or the Contractor/Co-publisher concerning the legal status of any country,
territory, city or area or of its authorities, or concerning the delimitation of its frontiers
or boundaries.

The designations 'developed' and 'developing' economies are intended for statistical
convenience and do not necessarily express a judgement about the stage reached by a
particular country, territory or area in the development process.

The views expressed herein are those of the authors and do not necessarily represent
those of IFAD.

Since 1974, Practical Action Publishing (formerly Intermediate Technology
Publications and ITDG Publishing) has published and disseminated books and
information in support of international development work throughout the world.
Practical Action Publishing Ltd (Company Reg. No. 1159018) is the wholly owned
publishing company of Practical Action. Practical Action Publishing trades only in
support of its parent charity objectives and any profits are covenanted back to Practical
Action (Charity Reg. No. 247257, Group VAT Registration No. 880 9924 76).

Cover photo: Women operate donkey-drawn plough in Sudan.
Credit: Annie Bungeroth/Practical Action
Cover design by Practical Action Publishing
Indexed by Andrea Palmer
Typeset by S.J.I. Services
Printed by Hobbs The Printers Ltd

Contents

Boxes and Tables

Boxes

Tables

Preface

Women are central to overcoming rural poverty. They play a critical role in poverty reduction and *food security* because they are responsible for both production and reproduction. Rural women in developing countries have longer working days than men because of their triple roles as farmers, caretakers of their families and cash earners through income-generating activities and microfinance. In addition, increasing drought and deforestation in many parts of the world make women's workload even more burdensome as they have to walk ever-longer distances to find firewood and clean water.

The multiple roles of women can act as an obstacle to development interventions, which often put additional pressure on women's time. Women's heavy workload reduces the time available for participation in project-related activities or affects their ability to care for their families. Ensuring women's access to labour-saving technologies for water, energy and farm-related activities is fundamental, and the need for such technologies is greater than it has ever been before.

This publication is timely. It looks back at three decades of experiences in introducing labour-saving technologies and practices to rural women and persisting gender discrimination in access and control. It also takes into account major developments in science, technology and innovation over the last several years and shows they can benefit women.

Gender equality and women's empowerment continue to be central to the mandate of the International Fund for Agricultural Development (IFAD). The key entry point for IFAD's engagement on the ground is the economic empowerment of poor rural women. It focuses on three critical and interrelated dimensions: expanding women's access to and control over fundamental assets such as capital, land, knowledge and technologies; strengthening women's decision-making role in community affairs and representation in local institutions; and improving women's well-being and easing their workloads by facilitating access to basic rural services and infrastructures. Through its projects, IFAD has experimented with a broad range of technological devices and practices aimed at strengthening women's access to water and energy, thereby easing their workload and improving the well-being of the whole family.

An initiative of the IFAD Technical Advisory Division, this publication will promote a better understanding and knowledge of labour savings technologies and practices and their implications on women and gender roles.

Acknowledgements

Marilyn Carr, international consultant on gender, technology, rural enterprise and poverty reduction, wrote this book in collaboration with Maria Hartl, technical adviser for gender and social equity in the IFAD Technical Advisory Division.

This publication is based on the authors' contribution on labour-saving technologies and practices in the *Gender in Agriculture Sourcebook* which was jointly produced by the World Bank, FAO and IFAD (2008).

The following people reviewed the content: Maria E. Fernandez (Center for the Integration of Research and Action, Department of Anthropology, University of North Carolina at Chapel Hill, USA), Clare Bishop-Sambrook (international consultant) and Ira Matuschke (University of Hohenheim, Germany).

The opinions expressed in this publication are those of the authors and do not necessarily represent those of the International Fund for Agricultural Development (IFAD). The designations employed here and the presentation of material do not imply the expression of any opinion whatsoever on the part of IFAD concerning the legal status of any country, territory, city or area or of its authorities, or concerning the delimitation of its frontiers or boundaries. The designations 'developed' and 'developing' countries are intended for statistical convenience and do not necessarily express a judgement about the stage reached by a particular country or area in the development process.

Acronyms

AT	appropriate technology
BRAC	Bangladesh Rural Advancement Committee
CA	conservation agriculture
CIDA	Canadian International Development Agency
FAO	Food and Agriculture Organization
GATS	General Agreement on Trade in Services
GRTI	Gender and Rural Transport Initiative
ICT	information and communications technology
IEA	International Energy Agency
IFAD	International Fund for Agricultural Development
IFPRI	International Food Policy Research Institute
ILO	International Labour Organization
IRRI	International Rice Research Institute
ITDG	Intermediate Technology Development Group
LPG	liquid petroleum gas
MDG	Millennium Development Goal
MHP	micro-hydro power
MSSRF	M.S. Swaminathan Research Foundation
NGO	non-governmental organization
NTAE	non-traditional agricultural export
TRIPS	trade-related intellectual property rights
UNDP	United Nations Development Programme
UNIFEM	United Nations Development Fund for Women
WUA	water user association

CHAPTER 1

Introduction

An African woman bent under the sun, weeding sorghum in an arid field with a hoe, a child strapped to her back – a vivid image of rural poverty. (World Bank, 2008a)

IN MOST DEVELOPING COUNTRIES, rural women's triple responsibilities of farm work, household chores and earning cash to supplement family incomes are well documented (World Bank, FAO, IFAD, 2008 b). The amount of time spent on each of these tasks and the way in which they are carried out varies from region to region and from country to country as well as within countries. The recent *World Development Report* talks of agriculture operating in three distinct worlds – one agriculture-based, one transforming and one urbanized (World Bank, 2008a). In agriculture-based countries (mostly in Africa), agriculture contributes a significant share of overall growth. In transforming countries (mostly in Asia), non-agricultural sectors dominate growth but a great majority of the poor are in rural areas. And in urbanized countries (mostly in Latin America, Europe and Central Asia), the largest number of poor people live in urban areas, although poverty rates are often highest in rural areas (ibid.). However, in all of these worlds, women's triple tasks often add up to a 16-hour day.

In agriculture-based countries (and agriculture-based regions within other countries) men, even from poorer families, now have access to improved technologies for use in farming and non-farm enterprise activities, but most women still struggle through their days using traditional technologies that are labour intensive and time and energy consuming. In these countries, which form the basis of this review, domestic chores such as collection of water and fuel wood divert women's time away from farming tasks and non-farm enterprise activities. Women's time poverty and lack of access to improved technologies and techniques lead to low agricultural yields and low levels of food security.

There is a wide range of technologies and techniques that could help address some of women's labour constraints. These include: improved stoves, rainwater harvesting schemes and intermediate transport devices that can reduce the time women spend on domestic chores such as collection of fuel wood and water; improved hoes, planters and grinding mills that can increase the productivity of their farming tasks; improved techniques such as conservation agriculture that can reduce the time needed for labour-intensive tasks such as weeding; and cassava graters, oil-seed presses and other food processing equipment that can help them earn more income in less time and/ or with less effort.

Members of the Mwieri Kirinyaga Women's Group carry firewood in Kenya. Carrying firewood is one of the most fatiguing and time-consuming tasks that rural women are responsible for.

Over the past 30 years, there have been countless development programmes and projects aimed at reducing women's time poverty by increasing their access to such labour-saving or productivity-increasing technologies and practices, but women are still overburdened. In fact, in many agriculture-based countries, the situation is getting worse. Rapid rates of deforestation and widespread droughts mean women have to walk longer distances to collect fuel wood and water. Rural to urban migration of men increases the farm work that women must undertake. Drought and disease reduce the numbers of draught animals available for farming and transport activities, and the spread of HIV and AIDS reduces the number of adults able to engage in agriculture. In some parts of sub-Saharan Africa, levels of food security are only four months in female-headed households and two months in households headed by orphans and grandparents, as compared with eight months in married households (Bishop-Sambrook, 2003).

This review looks at experiences in introducing labour-saving technologies and practices to rural women and examines the challenges involved and lessons that can be learned for more effective implementation. It draws on the projects and studies of the International Fund for Agricultural Development (IFAD) and other international organizations working on rural development that see the economic empowerment of rural women as a way of meeting the Millennium Development Goals (MDGs), and particularly Goal 1 (reducing by half the proportion of people living in extreme poverty by 2015). It does this within the context of the rapid global economic, environmental and socio-cultural changes that have been taking place over the last three decades.

It also takes into account the major changes that have been occurring in science, technology and innovation. These relate not only to the advent of the so-called 'new' technologies – information and communication technologies (ICTs), biotechnology and nanotechnology – but also new approaches to the ways in which science and technology are done. In particular, over the last 30 years, there has been a move away from introducing technologies to rural women towards participatory technology development that seeks to incorporate women's perspectives and, most recently, the development of women's innovative and technological capabilities to enable them to better solve their own problems in response to the rapid changes taking place around them.

This booklet is aimed at development planners and practitioners concerned with issues of poverty reduction and food security in the world's poorest countries – particularly the countries of sub-Saharan Africa. It highlights how economic and environmental policies, gender-sensitive planning and programming, and strategies aimed at introducing appropriate technologies and practices to rural women all have a role to play in this process. In so doing, it seeks to bring about a better integration of the work of those concerned with food production, informal rural industrialization, women's economic empowerment, environment and climate change, and the development and diffusion of science and technology.

CHAPTER 2
Women's workload in a changing global context

THE RAPID CHANGES in the economic, natural and socio-cultural environment within which rural women struggle to provide for themselves and their families have far-reaching implications for the linkages between women's workload, their access to labour-saving and productivity-increasing technologies, and levels of food production, food security, health and poverty.

Economic changes

Privatization and economic globalization have had a major impact on women's livelihoods in both the farm and non-farm sectors. On the positive side, new jobs have been created for women through the growth of non-traditional agricultural exports (NTAEs), and there are new opportunities for women farmers to supply the rapidly increasing numbers of supermarkets at home. There are also growing export markets for health and beauty products, which tend to be based on raw materials traditionally collected and used by women. On the negative side, however, women's labour has been diverted from food production to providing free labour on cash crops for export; and many of the small women's enterprises that were supported through the development of small-scale appropriate technologies in previous decades have suffered as a result of import competition (Carr and Chen, 2004; Carr and Marjoram, forthcoming). Moreover, many new jobs in NTAEs are of poor quality, and the support that rural women need to take advantage of new markets at home and globally has tended to be limited. In particular, the improved technologies that could help them to enhance the quality of their products and to diversify into growing markets have often not been available to them. This includes ICTs, which have spread rapidly in recent years and offer a new way of gaining access to information about production technologies as well as to business and market information, but which are much less accessible to women than to men.

At the same time, services that were previously provided through the state at highly subsidized rates – everything from water, sanitation and health services to tractor hire services and grid electricity – have now been increasingly privatized in the name of greater efficiency. In general, the result has been one of better services for the rich and worse or no services for the poor who cannot afford to pay for them. The literature abounds with examples of the failure of private water, sanitation and electricity delivery schemes to bring

Credit: M. Millinga/IFAD

Mobile phones are a new and powerful tool in rural marketing that are revolutionizing how women get information.

any improvements for the poorest segments of populations even in urban and peri-urban areas, and doubts are expressed that they will ever reach remote rural areas that are perceived as being high risk with low returns. Yet, despite this evidence and its implications for reaching many of the MDGs, the process of privatization is likely to be intensified in coming years as more countries sign up these basic needs sectors to the General Agreement on Trade in Services (GATS) (Mehta and Madsen, 2005).

Unfortunately, this is likely to be at the expense of investments in alternative, decentralized and community-driven schemes based on low-cost technologies that often are more suited to meet the needs and pockets of the rural poor. In fact, according to some researchers, liberalization of basic services through GATS could well lead to the breakdown of community-owned and operated schemes that have already been put in place (Thomas et al., 2007). The people most likely to suffer from this trend are rural women who, in the absence of electricity, convenient and safe sources of water, adequate sanitation facilities and accessible and affordable health care, will continue to spend a large part of their day in collecting water and fuel wood and caring for the sick – a way of life that is simply not sustainable.

Environmental changes

Increasing drought in many parts of the world is resulting in greater pressure on securing water. Rapidly increasing deforestation is making it more difficult to find firewood and to gain income from non-timber forest products. Increasing energy costs make it less likely that households will switch from female-intensive systems of energy provision to alternative sources, and there are growing shortages and rising costs of biomass fuels on which many of women's traditional non-farm activities depend. In addition, drought is a major cause of the death of draught animals, which have been used to provide a large part of farm power in the past and must now be substituted with human labour – much of which must come from already over-burdened rural women. Some developments, such as substitution of fossil fuels by biofuels, are creating as many problems as they solve and leading to debates about food versus fuel (Raswant et al., 2008; Rossi and Lambrou, 2008).

Women's access to labour-saving technologies for water, energy and farm-related activities obviously need to be considered within these new parameters. On the one hand the increasing pressures of drought and deforestation on women's time mean that the need for such technologies is greater than it has ever been before, but these same pressures are precisely the ones that reduce family income and make it difficult to invest in such technologies. On the other hand, the increased focus on the environment and climate change is leading to a renewed interest in the identification and diffusion of low-cost, labour-saving technologies that can help rural poor women to cope with these changes and in more investment in pro-poor and gender-sensitive science and technology.

Socio-cultural changes

Health issues are playing a greater role in agricultural programming as a result of increasing rates of malnutrition and ill-health in general, and the spread of HIV and AIDS in sub-Saharan Africa in particular. Women's workload both in domestic and in farming activities is affected in a number of ways. First, as women have the major responsibility for caring for the sick, their workload increases with higher rates of sickness and the corresponding decline of health-care services as a result of privatization. Second, malnutrition caused by a lack of food security means that women's productivity in farming and non-farming activities is much reduced.

Third, and, especially in Africa, the decimation of the adult male population as a result of AIDS is decreasing the already scarce labour supply in rural areas. In parts of sub-Saharan Africa, it is thought that between 10 and 20 per cent of the agricultural labour force are affected by HIV and AIDS (Bishop-Sambrook, 2003). This is bringing about a change in the division of labour in the household as women take over farming tasks that used to be carried out by men – a change that is being intensified by male migration to urban areas as it becomes increasingly difficult to make a living in rural areas. While this increases women's burden, it also has the potentially beneficial effect of breaking down taboos (such as women in Africa not being able to work with oxen) that have previously restricted women's productivity (ibid.). In addition, the focus on HIV and AIDS has reawakened interest in the issue of technologies that can release women's time from domestic chores so that it can be used in farming and other more productive activities. Many of the large donors, such as the Bill & Melinda Gates Foundation, that previously had a narrow focus on HIV and AIDS (and other major diseases such as malaria) are now incorporating funding for labour-saving technologies for rural women in their programmes. For example, the Foundation recently awarded a $19 million grant to a project in West Africa supported by the United Nations Development Programme (UNDP) that is designed to boost the productivity and income of women farmers using low-cost, mechanized power (UNDP, 2008).

Measures that could reduce the incidence of sickness and malnutrition in rural areas would have an immediate effect in terms of reducing women's workload. Some, such as those that bring clean water closer to the household or improve sanitation, have already been mentioned above. Others would include the provision of low-cost drugs – and especially those that help to reduce the effects of HIV and AIDS. The battle to increase access to cheap drugs in developing countries is still being fought – often in the face of changes in trade policy, such as the introduction of trade-related intellectual property rights (TRIPS), that exacerbate the situation. Even when cheap drugs are available, rural areas of most developing countries lack the health facilities needed to get these to the poor on the scale needed (see Chaudhuri, 2007).

CHAPTER 3

Impacts of labour-saving technologies on women's triple responsibilities

RURAL WOMEN in developing countries divide their time between domestic, farming and non-farm activities. The proportion of time allocated to each of these broad categories varies between and within regions, as well as between women in different types of households. In total, however, as noted earlier, most women in all regions work for approximately 16 hours a day. This is more than the number of hours worked by men, and a greater proportion of women's total work hours is spent on unpaid activities (see United Nations Statistical Division, 1995/2000/2005; UNDP, 1995).

Domestic chores

Tasks such as water and firewood collection, cooking, cleaning and child and health care take up inordinate amounts of women's time (World Bank, FAO and IFAD, 2008). Numerous programmes and projects, some of which are described in the following sections, have been introduced with the aim of improving the access of rural populations to water and energy supplies, as well as providing infrastructure such as roads and health clinics aimed at increasing mobility and access. However, the time spent on these tasks is still a major factor diverting women's labour away from farming tasks and income-generating activities.

Interventions aimed at reducing the time spent by women on domestic chores fall into two categories. These are:

- integration of women's needs into mainstream infrastructure projects; and
- projects aimed at delivering time- and energy-saving technologies directly to women.

Water supplies

Many water supply projects refer to the role of women in water provision and have singled them out as major beneficiaries, and yet it is estimated that 1.1 billion people – one person out of every six in the world – do not have access to safe water, and that 280,000 people worldwide need to gain such access every day between now and 2015 to reach the MDG target. Statistics for sanitation reveal an even worse situation, with 2.6 billion people (40 per cent of the world's population) having no access and with the need to reach 384,000 people each day by 2015 (Redhouse, 2005). It is women who bear the major brunt of these shortfalls – both in terms of time wasted in walking to and queuing at distant water sources, and in terms of caring for sick children suffering from diarrhoea and other water-borne diseases. The Human Development Report for 2006 estimates that women still spend 40 billion hours a year in water collection in sub-Saharan Africa alone (UNDP, 2006).

Mainstream approaches: piped water supplies

Although piped water is now reaching some people in the rural areas of developing countries, it is highly unlikely that it will ever reach more than a fraction of remote communities in the foreseeable future. Apart from the physical difficulties in providing high-technology solutions in rural areas, the resources required to meet the MDGs in terms of drinking water and sewage through such means would be enormous. The estimates for one country – Peru – are $2.9 billion and $1.1 billion for drinking water and sewerage respectively. Governments' budgets and development aid targeted for water supplies are hopelessly inadequate and falling, and the funds available are biased in favour of the better off. At the global level, less than 40 per cent of development aid for water goes to the 30 countries where nearly 90 per cent of the 1.1 billion people without access to safe water live. And within countries, it is normal to spend as much or more on the water supply and sewerage systems of the capital city than is allocated for the needs of the whole of the rest of the country (Redhouse, 2005).

Bottom-up approaches: decentralized water systems

Given the impossibility of meeting the water supply needs of rural communities through conventional means, the only alternative is to support the efforts of these communities to provide for themselves. There are many decentralized water systems based on rainwater harvesting, solar pumps, spring protection and other small-scale techniques and technologies that have the potential to make significant contributions towards meeting the MDGs in respect of access to safe drinking water. These are based on communities constructing, owning, operating, maintaining and repairing their own water schemes. Sometimes communities mobilize themselves; in other cases, they are mobilized around water issues by development agencies, local authorities or non-governmental organizations (NGOs), from whom they receive varying amounts of financial and technical support.

The involvement of rural women in these community-owned and operated schemes has been significant, and they have benefited from them both practically (in terms of time savings and improved hygiene) as well as strategically (in terms of increased voice and control). However, two factors have been identified that limit the extent of women's contributions and benefits. First, women are often under-represented on the water user

Credit: Sarah Nimeh/IFAD

Protected wells and other improved technologies help women with the task of water collection.

associations (WUAs) that make decisions on water schemes; and second, the payment required by WUAs (in cash or in kind) for the use of water is often beyond the means of very poor women (see Box 1).

According to a recent IFAD study on 'Gender and Agricultural Water Management', although tens of thousands of WUAs have been created worldwide in the last decade, women do not have an equal voice in water management (Wahaj, 2007). Lack of adequate representation on WUAs can mean that it is men's priorities in terms of location and use of water supplies that are reflected, and these are often different from those of women. For example, supplies can be allocated to irrigation (men's priority) while women still have to walk long distances to collect water for domestic purposes (Clancy and Kooijman, 2006). One reason for women's lack of voice is that because the multiple uses of water are not fully recognized and domestic uses are rarely seen as being as important as irrigation, it is felt that they have little or no reason to be involved in decisions about its management. Another is that membership is normally restricted to registered landowners, who very often are men (Wahaj and Hartl, 2007; Wajaj, 2007). But a major constraint on women's participation in planning bodies is their lack of time – in part caused by the distances they have to walk to collect water, the very problem they need to have a say in solving.

As recognition is increasing of the multi-purpose, multi-use and multi-user nature of water supply projects so is recognition of the importance of increasing the membership of women on WUAs. In some cases, affirmative action such as establishing a minimum quota for women has been introduced. However, it is often the better-off women who have greater amounts of time available to them who can take advantage of these quotas, and they are

---

Box 1: Women and community-based water schemes

The nine-year IFAD-supported Central Dry Area Smallholder and Community Services Development Project started operation in Kenya in 2001 with the objective of reducing poverty through the provision of social and physical infrastructure. The project relies on community-based action to ensure sustainability, and water user associations (WUAs) have been established that own, operate and maintain water supply facilities. Women have been major beneficiaries. The amount of time they spend in collecting water has been reduced from about half a day to only minutes through schemes such as construction of protected springs close to the village. Water quality is also much improved. Time is spent instead on kitchen gardens and rearing of cows and goats for milk that is sold for cash, and women no longer have to withdraw their daughters from school to help them fetch water. One problem is that the contribution requirements set up by the WUAs are often too high for the poorest women, who are then excluded. In addition, women make up only 29 per cent of the members of the WUAs, mainly because membership is registered in the name of the male head of household who owns the land. (*Source:* IFAD, 2006a.)

Women fix a water pipe used for irrigation in Mae Phrik, Thailand.

unlikely to be familiar with the needs and problems of the majority of rural women (Wahaj, 2007).

Although measures to increase women's voice in the planning and running of community water schemes need to continue, there is also a place for directly mobilizing women's groups around water issues. The extent to which women gain empowerment through such schemes can be much greater than through involvement in community WUAs (see Box 2), but they reach fewer women and hence have a smaller impact overall.

While communities and women's groups can contribute their own labour and cash to rural water schemes, there is still obviously a huge need for

---

Box 2: A women-controlled water scheme

During 1981–1994, Utthan (a large Indian NGO) supported the emergence of a community-based group called Mahiti based in Gujarat. Together they have initiated a women's movement focused around the issue of access to a safe and regular supply of drinking water. At the time, providing drinking water to remote communities through pipelines was the only accepted public distribution system. However, the women pressured the Gujarat Water Supply and Sewerage Board to approve a project that sought to promote decentralized rainwater harvesting structures such as plastic-lined ponds and roof water collection tanks. The women have gained empowerment through this process to the extent of lobbying district authorities to warn off neighbouring villagers who have attempted to steal their hard-won water supplies. (*Source:* Utthan Development Action Planning Team, 2001.)

financial and technical support from local and national governments, donor agencies and NGOs. If women's time spent on collecting water is not counted and valued, then the incentive to fund improved water supplies – either piped or decentralized – is reduced. Several studies, therefore, have focused on measuring the ways in which women use the time saved by labour-saving technologies. The 2006 Human Development Report provides an example from the Self Employed Women's Association (SEWA) in Gujarat, which estimates that, in the dry season, reducing the time spent by the average woman on water collection by one hour per day would result in up to $100 extra annual income per woman from craft production (UNDP, 2006). More facts and figures such as these are badly needed to make the case for investing in technologies that reduce the time rural women spend in water collection.

Rural energy

Rural communities need energy for a variety of purposes including cooking, lighting, heating, and powering farm and other production tools and equipment. Global poverty will be reduced only if there is energy to increase production, income and education, create jobs and alleviate the daily grind involved in just trying to survive. Decreasing hunger will not come about without energy for more productive growing, harvesting, processing and marketing of food. Improving health and reducing death rates will not happen without energy for the refrigeration needed for clinics, hospitals and vaccination campaigns. Children cannot study in the evenings without light in their homes. Clean water cannot be pumped or treated without energy, leaving families to face the risk of water-borne diseases; and the health of women and children will suffer while biomass continues to be used for cooking and heating, resulting in unsafe levels of indoor air pollution. All of this leads the United Nations Commission on Sustainable Development to conclude that 'to halve the proportion of people living on less than US$1 per day by 2015, access to affordable energy services is a prerequisite' (Thomas et al., 2007).

Mainstream approaches: grid electricity

Despite the important role of electricity in reducing poverty, over 1.6 billion people still lack access (27 per cent of the world's population). In South Asia only 40 per cent of the population has electricity, and in China – despite great strides having been made in rural electrification – over 70 million people remain without electricity, mostly in remote, sparsely populated areas. In sub-Saharan Africa, the number of households with access to electricity is only 22.6 per cent on average and falls as low as 7.2 per cent in Mozambique (Thomas et al., 2007). Wide discrepancies are observed between urban and rural areas. In Kenya, for example, the electricity grid supplies 40 per cent of urban households but less than 2 per cent of rural ones (Njenga, 2001). In most developing countries, the combination of a dispersed and relatively low level of demand for energy in rural areas and inadequate capital financing for widespread grid extension programmes means that many areas are unlikely to be connected to central power grids in the foreseeable future.

The International Energy Agency (IEA) estimates that over the next 30 years, investment in new power generating capacity will amount to $2.1 trillion, but this will still leave 1.4 billion people with no grid connection – most of them in rural areas. The IEA admits that private utilities will not extend networks to areas where it is unprofitable to do so, unless governments provide subsidies to meet the costs; yet, worldwide, governments are moving away from maintaining a publicly controlled energy sector towards increased liberalization and competition (Thomas et al., 2007; Misana and Karlsson, 2001).

While free trade advocates privatization as the only way of overcoming the inefficiencies inherent in state-controlled energy supply systems, there are alternatives that can provide shorter-term solutions to the need for energy in rural communities. These fall into three broad categories:

- use of improved wood and charcoal burning stoves for cooking and heating, which can reduce fuel consumption, indoor air pollution and carbon emissions as well as saving the time wasted by women on fuel wood collection;
- use of more efficient fuels for cooking and lighting; and
- introduction of decentralized rural energy/electricity systems that can be owned and operated by communities, groups and associations or individual entrepreneurs.

Improved wood and charcoal burning stoves

Half of the world's population and 80 per cent of rural households in developing countries cook with solid fuels such as wood, crop residues and dung. Fuel wood is collected free from surrounding forests or scrub areas and used by women in traditional open fires or in improved biomass stoves to cook meals and provide space heating. Along with the collection of domestic water supplies, the collection of fuel wood is one of the most time-consuming tasks undertaken by rural women – with the amount of time increasing as supplies become scarcer as a result of deforestation. The provision of fuel encompasses not only time spent in travelling, cutting and carrying, but also in preparation of fuel for burning and use, which can take more time than the actual collection itself. In addition, cooking on traditional stoves is a time-consuming business that requires constant attention and prevents women from engaging more fully in farming, income-generating activities and childcare. Studies show that increased fuel wood collection time corresponds directly with decreased time worked in agriculture. In addition, women have a set time for fuel collection and cooking, which means that the more time spent on collecting fuel wood, the less time is available for the actual cooking of the meal, resulting in poorer levels of nutrition (Cecelski, 2004). There is also evidence to show that the more time women spend on fuel wood collection, the less time they spend on the collection of water (ibid.).

Given the above, it is not surprising that a majority of energy projects aimed at benefiting women have focused on improved cook stoves. There have been some notable success stories along the way. These have included fuel-efficient wood-burning stoves such as the Lorena stove in India, the Upesi stove in East Africa and the Sarvodya stove in Sri Lanka – all of which have reached large numbers of rural women (Owala, 2001; Atukorala and Amerasekera, 2006).

The women who have acquired such stoves have undoubtedly benefited from their use in terms of time saved. For example, a study of Upesi stove users in Kenya found that there were time savings in fuel wood collection of about 10 hours per month, as well as fuel wood savings of up to 43 per cent compared with a three-stone stove (Njenga, 2001). Data on improved fuel wood stoves introduced in Sri Lanka shows that they reduced the time to cook one meal from 77 minutes with a traditional stove to 62 minutes (Carr and Sandhu, 1987). More advanced wood-burning stoves introduced in recent years have incorporated features that decrease indoor air pollution and thus have the added benefits of reducing health costs and the time spent by women on caring for children suffering from respiratory illnesses. The World Health Organization estimates that 1.6 million people a year (mainly women and children) die of health effects resulting from toxic indoor pollution. This has resulted in increased focus on the health aspects of cooking stoves and the design and dissemination of a range of 'rocket-type' chimney stoves, such as the ONIL stove, which improve on the older Lorena-type stove (Scott, 2005; Helps International, n.d.).

Perhaps one of the best known success stories is that of the Kenyan Ceramic Jiko stove, which is produced by hundreds of informal economy artisans (the metal cladding) and rural women potters (the ceramic liner). To date there are an estimated 2 million stoves in use, of which 780,000 are in Kenya where penetration is 16.8 per cent of all households (with highest penetration in urban areas). Although developed with the support of various NGOs in the 1980s, the stove has been sold without subsidy from the start. As production levels have increased, it has become much more affordable ($1–3 per stove) and its widespread use has saved millions of tons of charcoal (Walubengo, 1995).

However, despite hundreds of thousands of such projects worldwide, and allowing for some positive results, the most common way of cooking for the majority of rural women in agriculture-based countries remains a pot on top of three large stones and an open fire. A major barrier to the uptake of improved stoves is commonly thought to be women's lack of access to cash, and the unwillingness of their husbands to contribute cash when cooking can be undertaken free of charge on an open fire. Attempts by development projects and government programmes to solve the problem by distributing stoves at subsidized prices or free of charge have rarely proved successful and have often been counter-productive. For example, in Kenya, marketing efforts for the Upesi stoves were complicated by earlier subsidies that had allowed

Credit: Practical Action

A woman receives training making improved clay stoves in Sudan.

the government to distribute improved stoves without cost to users, thereby weakening later efforts to charge market rates (Njenga, 2001). And in India, a promising project based on distribution of stoves produced by local women potters collapsed when a government agency started to distribute free stoves produced from outside the local area (see Box 3).

Widespread uptake of improved stoves will require either that women have control of their own source of income or that their husbands can see sufficient

---

Box 3: How providing improved technologies free can be counter-productive

In one district of India, women potters had started making improved *chulas* (stoves), designed in collaboration with village women, and selling them for Rs 40 each (US$0.9). Although women really wanted these new *chulas,* they had no cash of their own and were afraid to ask their husbands for the full amount. Some pretended that the stoves cost only Rs 15 and were able to get this sum from their husbands, hoping to pay the remainder over a period of time. Development workers in the area worked out a system with the women and the potters that stoves would be subsidized at 50 per cent, with the idea that many more women would then be able to get the money from their husbands. In the process, it was felt that women would become more empowered and be able to open negotiations with their husbands on other issues of importance to them. However, before the scheme could take off, the state government started to distribute *chulas* made outside of the area free of charge. The local women potters lost their jobs, many of the free stoves were dismantled by husbands for their metal parts and a chance for a change in household dynamics was lost. (*Source:* Ghertner, 2006.)

---

economic benefits from the use of the stoves to warrant investing in them. As was the case with water supplies, any research findings that highlight the opportunity cost of the time women spend on collection of fuel wood and on cooking will contribute towards securing women's increased access to fuel-saving stoves.

However, there may also be a case for more innovative approaches to the marketing of improved wood and charcoal burning stoves. According to an article entitled 'Stove for the Developing World's Health' by Amanda Leigh Hagg in the *New York Times* of 22 January 2008, a recent joint venture by the Shell Foundation and the US-based enterprise Envirofit International aims to promote what it calls the first 'market-based model for clean-burning wood stove technology' to the developing world. Envirofit believes that 'hundreds of prior stoves projects were not guided by a real strategic vision of what it means to understand who the customer is, what they need and how to get it produced'. Its representatives have been visiting rural areas to study factors like the ergonomics of cooking habits and preferred colour schemes and, on the basis of the market research, the company will offer a variety of stoves including single or multipot, with and without chimneys, different colours and heights, and a range of prices from $10–200. It planned to work with local distributors to create rural supply chains that will include women making house calls in a variation of a 'Tupperware marketing strategy', and to start distributing 10 million stoves in 2008.

Diversification of fuel sources

Another way of reducing the amount of time women spend on fuel wood collection is to introduce improved stoves that utilize cooking fuels other than wood and charcoal. Some of these stoves, such as those using biogas, have been in use for some time and have gained widespread acceptance in countries such as China and India where there are high densities of both people and animals. Stoves using bottled gas or liquid petroleum gas (LPG) have become increasingly popular in oil-rich countries and among those who can afford the price of the fuel. And more recently, ethanol and/or methanol stoves are offering an alternative to LPG stoves. Methane, an alcohol produced worldwide on a vast scale from natural gas, can be produced much more cheaply than ethanol or kerosene, and in theory could be sold to the consumer at a lower price. As can be seen in Box 4, in

---

Box 4: A range of fuels for domestic cooking

The IFAD-supported West Guangxi Poverty Alleviation Project in China has involved the introduction of 2.73 million biogas tanks, which have been built by villagers. It is estimated that 7.65 million tons of standard coal and 13.4 million tons of firewood are saved annually. Similar IFAD-supported projects being set up elsewhere in China save women's time for more agricultural production as well as improving the living environment and producing high quality organic fertilizer. The Wulin Mountains Minority Areas Development Project includes a credit component aimed directly at women's income-generating activities, which increases the chances that time released by biogas stoves will be used to earn extra cash. (*Sources:* Dianzheng, 2007; Wang, 2007; IFAD, 2007b.)

An evaluation of LPG stoves in the Sudan found that after initial fears about the safety of LPG, women liked the new technology because it was cleaner and quicker than fuel wood stoves and easier to tend. Fuel costs per month were also cheaper than with fuel wood or charcoal. Despite this, many women stopped using their LPG stoves after a while and reverted to charcoal. One explanation is that currently LPG is available only in large containers that last for a full month. With no tradition of saving money on a daily basis in order to replace the containers, women have a cash flow problem when their containers are empty and revert to buying small amounts of charcoal on a daily basis – even though it ends up costing more. Efforts are now being made to promote a savings culture to overcome this problem. In addition, the private company that supplies LPG in the Sudan has realized that there is a potentially large market for its product in rural areas and is planning many innovations including better distribution systems, smaller containers and provision of credit to assist with stove purchases. (*Source:* Bates, 2007.)

Project Gaia deals with new fuels and stoves supplied on an industrial scale. It aims to bring alcohol-powered appliances, available in North America and Europe, to the developing world, powering them with ethanol or methanol. Dometic is an appliance manufacturer that has recently started looking at markets in developing countries and is currently setting up partnerships with those with capacity to supply fuels. Pilot studies are under way in Ethiopia (1,000 stoves), Nigeria (300 stoves) and South Africa (300 stoves) with the aim of demonstrating benefits and creating markets that can be satisfied by local producers of stoves and fuel. (*Source:* Stokes and Ebbeson, 2005.)

addition to saving women's time, these alternative stoves and fuels offer a number of advantages such as conserving forest resources, improving the kitchen environment through reduced smoke emissions and enabling cooking times to be better controlled so that meals can be served on time (and thus increasing harmony within the household). However, there are some challenges involved in their widespread use (see Box 4).

Decentralized electrification systems

Even though large numbers of rural communities will never be connected to the central grid, they are nevertheless able to secure many of the same benefits through connecting to decentralized grids. There is now significant evidence from around the developing world to show that decentralized, community-based schemes can provide electricity to many of the world's poorest people. Such schemes can be based on conventional energy sources such as diesel engines, which can support a mini-grid for lighting and electric pumps as well as powering a variety of end-use equipment such as grinding mills. However, with costs of fossil fuels rapidly increasing, there is a growing focus on systems based on renewable energy sources such as solar, wind, micro-hydro and biofuels.

Decentralized systems overcome many of the logistical and financial problems involved in connecting remote communities with electricity supplies (Box 5). While the technologies involved have proved to be viable on a pilot basis, there are numerous organizational and governance issues to be resolved if these systems are to reach sufficiently large numbers of people. In addition, in the case of biofuel generators, there are many questions to be asked as to the costs and benefits of growing crops for fuel versus food. The demand for biofuels is already having an impact on the prices for the world's two leading agricultural biofuel feedstocks: maize and sugar. The International Food Policy Research Institute (IFPRI) projects that maize prices will rise by more than 20 per cent by 2020 (and up to 71 per cent in a drastic expansion scenario), with food calorie levels decreasing significantly, especially in sub-Saharan Africa (von Braun, 2007). Similarly, a recent paper prepared for IFAD points out that 'the number of food-insecure people in the world would rise by more than 16 million for every percentage increase in the real prices of staple foods, meaning that 1.2 billion people could be chronically hungry by 2025: 600 million more than previously predicted'. However, under the right conditions biofuels could help mitigate climate change, reduce dependence on imported oil and save foreign exchange, benefit poor producers in remote areas where inputs are more expensive, and enable farmers to earn increased incomes by planting crops such as the *jatropha curcas* plant, an inedible oilseed bush, that do not compete with the production of food crops (Raswant et al., 2008; Rossi and Lambrou, 2008).

Box 5: Decentralized grid systems

In Nepal, due to very isolated settlements in the hills and mountains, electricity supplies through national grids are very costly. However, the same terrain creates enormous hydroelectric potential, which has led to the concept of micro-hydroelectricity projects to cater for local needs at relatively low costs. With the support of several NGOs and development agencies and the help of a favourable government policy environment, almost 1,600 micro-hydro power (MHP) plants were installed for rural electrification between 1962 and 2005 and some 45,000 new rural households per annum are now being provided with modern sources of energy. This technology has, to some extent, replaced traditional and time-consuming methods of agro-processing in many parts of rural Nepal as well as providing domestic energy sources, and the promotion of hydro electricity is expected to increase in future with the involvement of the private sector. Benefits to particular groups of the population such as women depend on the selection/choice of end-uses. For example, the addition of a grinding mill (which can reduce the time needed to process six gallons of mustard oil from ten days to one hour) would benefit women much more than a battery-charging station. About 70 per cent of MHPs are privately owned, leading to choices being based on effective demand for services and profit levels. In the 30 per cent of MHPs that are community owned, decisions and choices are made by management committees. Some MHPs do not have women on the management committee and, even where women were encouraged, technical issues were regarded as 'male' in most cases. Generally, males dominate the planning and initiation stages of the projects so their priorities are more likely to be taken into consideration. (*Source:* Bhattarai et al., 2006.)

In Mali, some 700 communities have installed biodiesel generators, powered by oil from the *jatropha*. The Malian Government is promoting cultivation of this bush to provide electricity for lighting homes, running water pumps and grain mills and other critical uses. The biodiesel is being used to replace diesel oil in generators attached to the multifunctional platforms that have been successfully supplying electricity to many villages in West Africa for a number of years. Quite a few of the development projects that support these mini-electricity systems (UNDP/IFAD; UNDP/Gates Foundation) respond only to requests from women's associations, which then own and operate the platforms. Mali hopes eventually to power all of the country's 12,000 villages with affordable, renewable energy sources. Similar programmes are being implemented in Burkina Faso and Senegal. (*Sources:* Practical Action, 2008; Burn and Coche, 2001.)

The Uganda Photovoltaic Pilot Project for Rural Electrification, funded by UNDP and the Global Environment Facility, has led to the installation of almost 600 solar home systems and over 40 institutional systems in rural areas that will remain off the national electric grid for at least 5 years. Benefits from home systems have included reduced drudgery in daily tasks, improved health conditions and greater opportunities for income generation. Benefits from institutional systems have included those in the area of health (e.g., refrigerators for vaccines and lights for maternity wards) and education (e.g., lights for night studies at secondary schools). Women entrepreneurs were encouraged to buy solar systems to improve their businesses, but this proved to be unsuccessful because of inappropriate credit arrangements. However, women have been trained along with men as solar technicians. (*Source:* Sengendo, 2001.)

Rural transport

Rural transport is closely related to the issue of collection of water and fuel wood. One way of easing the burden of women's work is to increase their access to carrying devices, often referred to as intermediate means of transport (IMTs) – such as donkeys, wheelbarrows and carts – as well as improving the paths and roads over which they must travel. As can be seen in Table 1, which is based on Tanzanian statistics, women are responsible for many other transportation tasks, all of which could be made easier through access to improved transport technologies.

Statistics similar to those in Tanzania are available from many other developing countries. They show that women and men in rural households have different transport tasks, and that women often carry a heavier burden in terms of time and effort spent on transport (Blackden and Wodon, 2006; Peters, 2001) However, with less access to and control over resources, they have fewer opportunities than men to use transport technologies that could alleviate their burden, and gender issues are still peripheral to much of rural transport policy and practice (Fernando and Porter, 2002).

Mainstream approaches: major roads programmes

A critical need in rural areas of many developing countries is for improved roads and tracks between homes and farms, grinding mills, forests, water sources, schools, health clinics and markets. Existing tracks and paths often preclude the use of any type of wheeled transport. However, rural transport projects often concentrate on providing major roads rather than on improving the small roads and tracks/feeder roads that most rural women (and men) use for local transportation. One possible reason for this is that women have rarely been included in the planning of transportation interventions. In recognition of this, the World Bank recently commissioned a series of ten country studies on 'Integrating Gender into World Bank Financed Transport Programs', and has incorporated the findings of such studies into projects such as the Peru Rural Roads Program (Box 6). In Uganda, a similar study found that road

Table 1. Transportation tasks in rural Tanzania: hours per annum

Task	Adult females	Adult males	Children
Water collection	587	32	68
Crop establishment	251	194	63
Crop weeding	99	76	25
Crop harvesting	91	64	23
Internal marketing	9	4	1
Health	73	25	0
Grinding mill	169	21	13
Trips to market	227	51	0
Total	1,842 (71.6%)	492 (19.1%)	239 (9.3%)

Source: Barwell and Malmberg Calvo, 1987.

Credit: Louis Dematteis/IFAD

A woman grinds wheat at a corn and wheat mill belonging to the Women's Solidarity group 'Las Tres Rosas' in the Cabañas Department. Good roads are needed to take such produce to market.

Box 6: Gender and the Peru Rural Roads Program

In the World Bank/Inter-American Development Bank Rural Roads Program in Peru, special attention was given to gender issues in the component that dealt with small roads and tracks, with separate sessions held for women in consultation workshops. Women talked of their heavy time burdens, cultural barriers to use of public transport and long distance travel, lack of funds and inability to access privately held modes of transport, and limited voice in previous transport interventions, which had resulted in their needs being ignored. Targets set for women were 20 per cent of members of road committees, 10 per cent of members of microenterprises set up to undertake road-related activities and 30 per cent of the direct beneficiaries in local development window projects aimed to help microenterprises carry out activities other than road maintenance. Qualifications for application were altered to include women's experience in managing households as management experience. As a result of the programme, women spend less time collecting fuel and food supplies and more time in local and political activities and in visiting markets. They feel they can travel further and more safely, which enables them to earn more income. Transport costs for both women and men have decreased by 50 per cent, and everyone in the communities enjoys better access to markets and health-care facilities. (*Source:* World Bank, 2004.)

construction, rehabilitation and maintenance were predominantly male-biased. The programme was accordingly designed to ensure that gender issues were addressed by all institutions, systems and structures engaged in the roads sub-sector (Tanzarn, 2003).

However, even the provision of more and better rural roads is not particularly helpful if there is no access to appropriate transport devices. Carrying heavy loads along a road may be better than struggling along a rough path, but only marginally so. In fact, according to a recent IFAD study in Uganda, where 75 per cent of journeys each day were found to be carried out on foot, road improvements actually made things worse for women by depriving them of tracks they had previously used and leaving them at risk of being run over (IFAD, 2007a).

Public transport systems are more common and cheaper in Asia than in Africa, where women have had very few alternatives available to them other than head loading/walking. Where such systems do exist in Africa, they provide a reasonably cheap way for women to travel to market or to health clinics, but they are not without their difficulties. In particular, women often get left behind or stranded along the route when preference is given to male customers or to those travelling further afield. Harassment and safety are major concerns for women travelling long distances alone. One group of women in Kenya solved this problem by registering as a cooperative to obtain a loan and then buying their own bus, which operates successfully as a profit-making enterprise and gives preference to women cooperative members (Kneerim, 1980).

Bottom-up approaches: intermediate means of transport

Improved roads make it possible to use a range of IMTs that would not be appropriate for use on rough rural paths. These include wheelbarrows, pushcarts, animal-drawn carts and bush ambulances. In theory, the use of IMTs can generate a significant reduction in the time and effort spent by women on transportation tasks. For instance, the use of a wheelbarrow with a payload of 50 kilograms compared with head-loading (20 kilogram capacity) can reduce the time spent on water transport by 60 per cent (Mwankusye, 2002).

However, there are a range of socio-cultural and economic barriers to women's access to such IMTs. Wheelbarrows are often rejected by women who are used to standing straight while head-loading and who find it physically distressing to bend and push these devices. Carts are expensive and often owned by men, who use them for their own purposes and do not provide their wives with access even when they have been distributed through development projects aimed at assisting entire rural households. And, using draught animals for farm activities and transport is often seen as a male activity, with training being given only to men.

An interesting aspect of IMTs is that they often result in a changing division of labour within the household. This is sometimes to women's advantage, but

Credit: Franco Mattioli/IFAD

Animal panniers and animal drawn carts can reduce the time needed to carry water and other commodities and also form the basis of an income-generating activity for women.

often it adds to their workload or deprives them of new economic opportunities (Box 7).

On-farm activities

Generally, the roles of men and women in farming are well defined, with men responsible for land clearing and preparation and women responsible for planting, weeding, harvesting and post-harvest activities such as threshing, winnowing and grinding. All of these tasks take up a great deal of time and energy that can be reduced in one of two ways:

- making existing tasks easier and increasing the productivity of existing labour and animal draught power; or
- changing farming practices to methods that reduce the demand for power.

Improving farm power

Improved technologies that can increase labour productivity in farming have mostly been adopted in relation to men's tasks – often with negative consequences for women. For example, tractors and animal-drawn ploughs have been used by men to increase the acreage under cultivation, leaving women to struggle with an increase in weeding and harvesting operations

Box 7: Transport technologies and changes in the division of labour

Many men who will not head-load water and fuel for cultural reasons are happy to transport these if they have access to an IMT. Some projects have actively supported this trend on the assumption that if men take over what used to be women's work, it will take some of the burden off women and release their time for more productive activities. While this does happen in some circumstances, there are also cases in which it is the potential money to be made in selling water and firewood that is attractive to the men, and they use the IMTs to run profitable enterprises. In one project in South Africa, the impact on women was actually negative as men collected firewood for commercial use from resources closest to the homestead, forcing women to travel even further to collect fuel wood for domestic use. (*Source:* Venter and Mashiri, 2007.)

In Tamil Nadu in India, women were trained to ride bicycles as part of a literacy campaign. Loans were made available, but only women with permanent jobs were able to use these to buy their own bicycle. Although most rural women now know how to ride, they have access only to their husband's bicycle and can only use this when it is convenient for him. This highlights the difference between access to and control over an asset. While access to bicycles has increased women's self-confidence and allowed them to become more involved in community activities as it is easier for them to travel from village to village, many also say that their workload has increased as their husbands now expect them to undertake tasks such as marketing and taking the children to school that were not possible when they were less mobile. (*Source:* Rao, 2002.)

Bicycles and motorbikes can open opportunities for women such as enabling their role as extension workers.

Credit: Anwar Hossain

using only hand-held tools. This not only adds to women's workload, but can also result in major crop losses if weeding is done late or there are labour constraints. Although many women now undertake men's tasks due to male migration or death due to AIDS, manufacturers and suppliers of farming equipment seem to be unaware of this changing division of labour and continue to distribute ploughs that are too heavy for women or have handles they cannot reach (IFAD Technical Advisory Division, 1998).

Tools and equipment appropriate for women's tasks such as planting, weeding and grinding do exist, but there are many barriers to their adoption. Of all women's tasks on the land, weeding with short-handled hoes is the most punishing and time-consuming, causing fatigue and backache. Long-handled hoes are available that could reduce the strain of squatting, but in many parts of Africa these are rejected for cultural reasons. Manufacturers of farm implements make different weights of hoes, including very light ones that are better suited to women's needs, but most women continue to use heavier hoes because they are unaware of the full range of available tools. Lighter implements suitable for use with donkeys are also available and, unlike with oxen, no taboos exist on women working with donkeys. A donkey-drawn inter-crop cultivator could reduce weeding time per acre from 2 to 4 weeks to 2 to 4 days, but women lack the cash to purchase such equipment and men see no need to purchase donkeys and equipment for their wives when the work can be done by hand at no cost. In addition, animal draught technologies are seen as being men's domain, and animal traction training courses tend to be restricted to men (IFAD Technical Advisory Division, 1998). Even when donkeys and equipment are distributed to women through development projects, constraints on sustained use arise such as women's inability to pay for drugs to keep their animals disease free (GRTI, 2006a).

Plastic drum seeders, which have been widely promoted through the International Rice Research Institute (IRRI) and others in South-East and South Asia, enable farmers to sow rice seeds directly instead of broadcasting or transplanting rice seedlings. These seeders have proved very popular with farmers as they lower production costs through reduced use of seeds and labour and give higher yields. Data from an IRRI project in Vietnam show the time spent by women on tasks such as gap-filling and hand-weeding are vastly reduced (see Table 2).

The seeders have proved popular with women from better-off households, who now have more time to spend on childcare, income-generating activities and community activities. Studies have found that 81 per cent of women from such households were able to decrease their labour inputs into gap-filling and hand-weeding and that 90 per cent were happy with the introduction of the seeders. However, the technology has resulted in the loss of livelihoods for the many women from poorer and landless households who used to be hired by farmers to undertake these tasks, with almost 50 per cent of poor women and 100 per cent of landless women losing their work opportunities on other farms. While most poor women were able to diversify their income-generating

Table 2. Labour inputs into rice crop production, by gender (person days/hectare)

Operation	Conventional broadcast method		Drum seeder	
	Women	Men	Women	Men
Land preparation	3.67	6.53	4.13	4.13
Seedbed preparation	0.57	0.70	0.53	0.57
Sowing	0.57	1.73	0.70	2.53
Gap-filling	14.17	10.03	8.33	4.03
Hand weeding	13.83	6.90	8.50	3.17
Fertilizer application	4.70	3.10	1.37	5.13
Pesticide application	0.63	5.40	0.90	3.93
Irrigation	1.17	3.67	0.67	3.87
Harvesting	19.03	26.40	12.50	13.67
Threshing and drying	13.80	14.97	12.33	17.57
Total	72.14	79.43	49.96	58.60

Note: numbers are calculated as a per year average, and they comprise three cropping seasons (e.g., Winter–Spring, Summer–Autumn and Autumn–Winter).
Source: adapted from Paris and Chi (2005).

activities or find work on more distant rice farms, only 56 per cent of landless women were able to do so. For both categories, most women stated that job losses and concomitant decreases in income led to shortages in food, and they perceived an increase in their poverty levels. Thus, labour-saving technologies may not be beneficial for all groups of women.

The drum seeders are now being transferred with IFAD support to Bangladesh, where tests are showing increased yields and net returns for farmers and the private sector is becoming involved in production to meet a potentially large and growing demand. While Bangladesh may present a different picture than Vietnam because of greater labour shortages in rice production, it is to be hoped that some of the lessons learned from the Vietnam experience can be used to plan for alternative income opportunities for any poor women who lose their jobs as a consequence of technical change (Paris and Chi, 2005).

Other improved technologies, such as grinding mills, cassava graters and oil expellers, are now to be found in almost every village in the developing world. Some of them are owned by community organizations and women's groups, but the majority are owned by individual entrepreneurs – mainly men. The rapid spread of these processing technologies has been fuelled by the increasing availability of energy supplies in rural areas and by the significant profits that can be made from operating rural processing enterprises. Rural mills and other crop-processing technologies cut the time involved in hand pounding or grating from several hours to only minutes and have undoubtedly improved the lives of millions of women (see Box 8).

However, two problems exist. First, the mills and other machines have opened up investment opportunities for men rather than for women who cannot afford to buy them. They also exclude those women from the poorest farm households, who cannot afford to pay for milling services. Attempts

---

Box 8: Labour and time-saving crop processing technologies

In Nepal, mechanized mills were found to reduce the time needed to process one kilo of rice from 19 minutes to 0.8 minutes, but women were walking for 10 to 180 minutes to reach the mill and waiting an average of 30 minutes for their turn. Such behaviour has been noted in many parts of Asia and Africa and suggests that women are more concerned with the energy savings than the time savings connected to mechanical crop processing. (*Source:* Intermediate Technology Development Group, 1986.)

In Botswana, sorghum mills reduced the time needed to process 20 kg of sorghum from 2–4 hours to 2–4 minutes. Pounding traditionally takes place in the evening whereas the mills operate only in the mornings. Women solved this problem by sending grain to the mill with their children on the way to and from school. (*Source:* Spence, 1986.)

---

have been made to overcome ownership problems by developing smaller and cheaper technologies that would be better suited to women's cash and credit resources. Frequently, these interventions have been counter-productive in that they have resulted in the introduction of equipment such as hand-operated cassava graters or maize shellers that do little if anything in terms of eliminating the drudgery element of women's work and have thus been rejected by women entrepreneurs and women users (see Table 3). However, there have been success stories. For example, a ram press for processing sunflower seed oil, which was introduced in Africa in the 1980s, was adapted several times by workshops in the informal sector in response to buyer demands and a number of versions are now on sale, including one that is low-cost, small and easily operated by one woman (Haggblade et al., 2007; Hyman, 1993).

When large numbers of women process crops for local farmers using traditional techniques, mechanized equipment can result in the loss of a valuable source of income with dire consequences if no alternative remunerative work can be found. Perhaps one of the best examples of this is the introduction of rural rice mills in Bangladesh that, during the 1980s, resulted in the displacement of about 100,000 women per year. One solution

Table 3. Comparative processing times of traditional, semi-mechanized and mechanized technologies

Operation	Time required to process 1kg of product (mins)		
	Traditional	Semi-mechanized (improved hand-operated)	Mechanized
Shelling maize	8–15	3–5	0.03
Milling maize	5	3	<0.05
Threshing rice	3	0.12–1.0	0.2
Dehusking rice	6–12	4	<0.012

Source: Cecelski, 1984.

can be to help women organize into cooperative groups and provide them with loans so that they can purchase their own mills and operate them for hire, thus sharing in the benefits of the new technology. This strategy was successfully implemented in Bangladesh by several of the larger NGOs such as Bangladesh Rural Advancement Committee (BRAC) (Ahmad and Jenkins, 1989). However, cooperative ownership does not work well in all cultures, and individually owned mills have proved more profitable in nearly all continents and countries than those owned and operated by groups.

Changing farming practices

While increasing access to farm power is one way of solving women's time and energy-constraints related to on-farm activities, it is also possible to reduce the demand for power through changing farming practices. A good example of this is the adoption of conservation agriculture (CA) or zero/minimum tillage agriculture, which overcomes the critical labour peaks of land preparation and weeding by planting directly into mulch or cover crops, with weed control being done either by hand or herbicides.

While IFAD, the Food and Agriculture Organization (FAO) and others have implemented projects to introduce such practices, along with new types of farm equipment such as jab planters, results have been mixed. In a CA project supported by FAO in Tanzania, yields increased and time spent on land preparation, planting and weeding was much reduced (see Table 4). Women in poor farm households benefited from a decrease in labour pressure, but women in landless households received fewer opportunities to work in planting and seeding – although this effect could be cushioned by higher labour requirements in harvesting if yields were sufficiently increased.

While greater yields are an incentive to the adoption of CA, it faces numerous challenges including cultural resistance to a farming system that keeps crop residues as soil cover and involves no-till practices – both of which are considered to be signs of laziness. In addition, while CA is no more expensive than conventional agriculture, it does involve the need for cash to purchase inputs up-front (Maguzu et al., 2007). Also, in regions such as

Table 4. Labour requirements with conservation and conventional agricultural practices in maize farming, Tanzania

Activity	Conservation agriculture			Conventional agriculture		
	Labour/Acre	Implement	Time/acre	Labour/acre	Implement	Time/acre
Land prep.	2–3 people	Ripper	3 days	2–4 people	Plough	3–4 days
Planting	2 people	Jab planter	2 days	3 people	Draught animals	3–4 days
Weeding	8–10 people perform once	Hand hoe	1 day	·8–10 people perform twice	Hand hoe	1 day

Source: Maguzu et al., 2007.

Latin America in which 'full CA' is practised, there is an increase in the use of chemicals, which represent a health hazard to the women who apply them. In Africa, lower amounts of herbicides are used as farmers still do some weeding, although less than in the case of traditional cultivation (Matuschke, 2007).

A joint study by IFAD and FAO focused on vulnerable households in two districts of Tanzania and on two principle components within CA: reduced tillage and cover crops (RTCC). Although RTCC falls short of the integrated approach of CA (with simultaneous practice of permanent soil cover, minimal soil disturbance and crop rotation), each element represents a step towards CA. The findings from the study suggest that it is possible to make significant savings in labour inputs with RTCC technologies and practices by enabling particular tasks to be undertaken in a shorter time, and it also requires fewer people to operate and fewer draught animals. Who benefits from these labour savings was found to be household and/or gender specific. For example, men benefit from time saved with using draught animals or tractors more efficiently. Women benefit from draught animal-related technologies that reduce planting activities (such as the no-till planter or the ripper planter); and women also benefit from any reduction in the time spent weeding. The jab-planter and draught animal no-till planter were rated highly by farmers due to their labour-saving attributes, ease of use (women particularly appreciated not having to bend over to plant) and ability to penetrate trash. However, both were perceived to be expensive in comparison to conventional tillage implements. The study concludes that while land degradation has played a crucial role in sparking an interest in elements of CA, it may take the impact of HIV and AIDS and severe labour shortages to act as the catalyst for change, propelling African smallholders down the path of RTCC towards CA (Bishop-Sambrook et al., 2004).

Off-farm activities

A major objective of projects that introduce labour-saving technologies and practices is to help women divert time from subsistence farming activities and domestic chores into more productive income-generating enterprises. Often, the most remunerative of these activities – and particularly those related to food processing – are themselves intensive in their use of water and/or fuel wood and involve laborious production and processing methods using traditional techniques and technologies. This can require quantities of women's time that simply may not be available to them. In some circumstances, increasingly scarce water supplies and rising costs of fuel can threaten the existence of women's traditional food processing industries unless they are able to gain access to improved technologies and practices. Rural women need labour-saving technologies to increase the productivity of the time they spend in their microenterprise activities. They also need assistance to diversify into the production of some of these technologies as a way of increasing their off-farm income.

Labour-saving technologies and practices

Brewing is a major source of income for many women in sub-Saharan Africa. It accounts for up to 25 per cent of total wood fuel consumed by the household and requires time-consuming energy management to prevent losses through over-fermentation or failure to ferment. Interventions have included design and dissemination of improved stoves for home brewing in the expectation that women would be willing and able to invest in these if they result in lower costs of production. But continuous fire management affects fuel efficiency relatively more than technology design – a fact that has often been missed by development projects that have failed to consult adequately with women entrepreneurs (McCall, 2001). Innovative practices that break with tradition and establish cooperative brewing enterprises using larger scale technologies could well provide a more satisfactory solution.

When rural women are properly consulted and involved in the design and adaptation process, there can be significant benefits for those involved in food processing enterprises, as well as for artisans involved in the production and sale of the improved technologies on which they are based (see Box 9).

Often women have come up with their own innovative solutions to shortages of the raw materials or fuel supplies on which their traditional industries depend. For example, in Nigeria, women have traditionally processed locust beans to make *daddawa* – a savoury powder made from local ingredients in West Africa – that is regularly added to soups and stews to give flavour and extra protein. Women play a major role in the processing and

Two Sri Lankan women holding large basket of dried fruit, which has been processed and packaged by a small enterprise.

Box 9: Women's role in innovation in West Africa

Most women in the coastal areas of West Africa make a living through smoking and selling fish. In the 1980s, in collaboration with women users, a local technology institute in Ghana (Food Research Institute) developed an improved oven that is now in widespread use throughout the region. The new oven enables women to undertake three smoking cycles a day, while only one cycle was possible with the traditional technology. Most women spend the same time processing more fish, rather than spending less time on smoking the same amount of fish. Even so, there are still some time savings as the new technology is easier to operate and allows women to tend to other household tasks while fish is being smoked. Women also have more time to engage in social and community activities. One unexpected consequence of this successful technology has been that profits increased to such an extent that men began to take over what has traditionally been a women's industry and to compete with them. More recently, also in consultation with women entrepreneurs, a UNIFEM-supported project has enabled the GRATIS Foundation to develop a fish smoker that depends only on gas (LPG) for fuel, thus solving problems of smoke inhalation that previous improved ovens did not deal with. (*Sources:* International Labour Organization/ Netherlands Government, 1985; Sandhu, 1989; Mensah, 2001.)

In Nigeria, one of the most time-consuming aspects of preparing *gari* – a convenience food made from cassava – is that of grating the tubers, which can take a whole day using traditional manual technologies. A mechanized grater was developed by an artisan carpenter in Benin State at the behest of his three wives, and the original prototype has been adapted by local artisans over time in response to the suggestions of female users. Time spent on grating is reduced from one day to around 15 minutes. However, women cannot afford to own the graters they helped to design, and most are owned by men – who hire female operators. Thus, although the graters lead to a reduction in the time women spend on grating cassava (time that they divert mainly to other economic activities such as making more *gari* and engaging in retail trade), they do not benefit from profits on the grating process, and the profit made from *gari* processing (as opposed to grating) is very small. (*Source:* Adjebeng-Asem, 1990.)

---

marketing of *daddawa,* which provides many thousands of them with a source of income. When locust beans became difficult to secure from the wild due to land being diverted to cash crops, women substituted soybeans as the raw material. They are able to grow these in their fields instead of having to secure locust beans from trees that normally grow on land to which men hold the user rights. In addition, the cooking time of soybeans is about 25 per cent of that for locust beans, thus reducing the requirement for fuel wood. Knowledge about soybean growing and processing has spread from woman to woman by word of mouth, and knowledge has been freely shared with neighbouring communities and enterprises – thus highlighting the important role of peer training and exchange of information among women in the process of technology transfer (Ilkarracan and Appleton, 1995).

Labour and energy saving technologies as a basis for women's enterprises

The increasing demand for time- and energy-saving technologies can in itself form the basis for income-generating activities for women. Examples of energy entrepreneurs include women making stoves in Kenya, installing solar systems in India and manufacturing and selling lamps in Bangladesh and Peru. In Malawi women are making biomass briquettes for sale, and in Mali they are operating diesel generators as businesses and selling energy services (see Box 10).

Box 10: Women as energy entrepreneurs

In Kenya, rural women potters have been helped by an NGO to diversify into stove production to meet the energy needs of their community and increase their incomes. Women are now producing thousands of improved wood-burning stoves as well as ceramic liners for jiko charcoal-burning stoves, and they have developed and maintained linkages through which these are marketed. Some of the more innovative women have designed new types of stoves to meet the particular needs of local women. (*Sources:* Owala, 2001; Njenga, 2001.)

In India, illiterate women from eight states have been trained as 'barefoot solar engineers' to establish solar energy systems in areas where electricity supply is either non-existent or highly erratic They install solar systems in even the most remote places, where people are now able to use solar energy for heating, water supply and other activities. (*Source:* Gupta, 2007.)

In Peru, with the help of a local NGO, women have adapted a type of light that uses combustible vaporized kerosene to replace candles. Having tested various types of containers, they worked out a design using empty cans of evaporated milk and, little by little, they developed the tools needed to produce the lamps. Both the materials and the tools cost virtually nothing. Women now produce and market a profitable product and also earn income from craftwork undertaken during the evening hours with the benefit of the new lamps. (*Source:* Appleton, 1994.)

In Mali, with support from a UNDP/IFAD regional project and many other local and international agencies, women are operating diesel generators as businesses and selling energy services. These enterprises are based on a multifunctional platform that consists of a small diesel engine mounted on a chassis to which a variety of end-use equipment can be attached, including grinding mills, battery chargers, vegetable or nut oil presses, welding machines and carpentry tools. It can also support a mini grid for lighting and electric pumps for a small water distribution network or irrigation system. The platform was purposely designed to take into account the multiple end uses for energy in rural economies and to provide a substitute for human energy. Although these platforms were already being used in various countries in Africa, support from the UNDP/IFAD project is conditional on use being managed by women's associations. (*Source:* Burn and Coche, 2001.)

Most of these enterprises result in significant income gains, but there are many other benefits. In particular, local communities are highly appreciative of being able to have light in the evenings or save on the amount of fuel wood needed for cooking and heating. As a result, in addition to contributing to the wealth and well-being of their communities, the women involved in such activities command a good deal of respect and their self-esteem is much increased (Misana and Karlsson, 2001).

There are also opportunities for operating profitable businesses through collecting and selling water and fuel wood using various types of intermediate transport devices. As seen above, men seem to monopolize such businesses when their profitability is assured. However, there are several examples of women running successful transportation businesses and even innovating and adapting in response to changing environments (see Box 11).

Finally, if enabled to do so, women can also find work and gain income in the construction and maintenance of rural infrastructure such as roads and water supply systems. A major example of this is the Rural Maintenance Programme (RMP) in Bangladesh, which has improved the standard of living of thousands of destitute women through employment in routine maintenance systems for earthen farm-to-market roads. Established in the 1980s as a Canadian International Development Agency (CIDA) bilateral infrastructure project, the programme's later phases have included components to provide women with the necessary skills so that they can earn a living when they leave the project and not return to destitution. According to an independent review in the mid-1990s, this objective was achieved in the case of 70 per cent of the programme's graduates (McCann, 1998).

Box 11: Women investing in transport

In the suburbs of a rural town in Mali, a group of women, exhausted by the amount of time they spent each day collecting clean water, organized themselves to acquire a donkey and cart with the support of an NGO, which also provided them with training to manage the enterprise. This reduced their own workload, as well as that of neighbouring women, and generated savings to invest in other activities. After a while, a water supply network was installed, so now they use their carts to collect household refuse. (*Source:* GRTI, 2006b.)

CHAPTER 4
Where are we now?

The macro picture

Since the early 1970s, there has undoubtedly been widespread dissemination of labour-saving technologies and practices. To the extent that these have reached rural women, they have contributed towards achieving the objectives of the MDGs, and especially that of poverty reduction. However, there are still large numbers of rural women in agriculture-based countries and regions who must grow and process food without access to improved technologies and techniques and who must spend long hours collecting fuel wood and water – time that could far more productively be spent in food production and income-generating activities.

Although much still needs to be done in terms of increasing the access of these women to existing improved technologies, the recent revival of interest in science and technology for development within the United Nations and elsewhere has tended to focus on the so-called 'new technologies' – ICTs, biotechnology and nanotechnology. The assumption is that these will have a widespread impact on poverty in developing countries through meeting objectives such as increasing food production and reducing rates of malnutrition, providing safe water and sanitation, and increasing the supply of low-cost drugs tackling HIV and AIDS, tuberculosis and malaria. In certain circumstances, however, some of these objectives could be met at lower cost using more 'traditional' technologies. Yet, these more traditional technologies receive very little attention, and inadequate funding is allocated to achieving their uptake on a more widespread basis. As a result, in some very poor countries such as Bangladesh, while up to a third of the population have access to mobile phones (Shaffer, 2007), less than one tenth have access to safe drinking water and sanitation. In other countries, attempts are being made to introduce nanotechnology to filter out impurities in rural water supplies when the communities concerned, if asked and if supported to do so, could come up with several less expensive and more appropriate ways of doing this (Grimshaw, 2007).

In its 2008 report on *Global Economic Prospects,* the World Bank (2008b) examines the major issues involved in technology diffusion in developing countries. It concludes that while technology is spreading to developing countries through foreign trade and investment and through migration, most of these countries have not been good at putting it into widespread use. Improved access to better water and sanitation and energy services is highly concentrated in urban areas while resources to upgrade services and provide access to improved technologies in rural areas are totally inadequate. While technologies that gain a foothold in developed countries go on to reach the majority of the population, in developing countries they are less likely to catch on and those that do so spread much less quickly (with the exception, as noted above, of mobile phones). It also points out that one of the major constraints on the spread of 'new technologies' is the failure to adopt 'old technologies'. For example, electricity is needed to run computers and provide the refrigeration necessary to spread the benefits of new health technologies and breakthroughs in modern health care. But electricity is still a rare commodity in most rural areas in developing countries.

Statistics on the use of 'new' technologies tend to be well recorded. For example, we have a fairly accurate picture of the numbers of people in developing countries who have access to computers and mobile phones (International Telecommunications Union, 2007). In addition, increased concern with equity and poverty reduction in recent years is leading to a more careful disaggregation of data on these technologies by rural and urban areas and by women and men – although this is not being done systematically and far more work is needed (Huyer et al., 2005).

The same is not true of the 'older' technologies such as water pumps and grinding mills. While we have a general picture of the significant but insufficient spread of such technologies over the last 30 years, we do not know the numbers actually available per person in rural areas in particular countries, or how many women and men own, control and use them. It could be useful to examine the information available from agricultural surveys, census data, case studies and project reports such as those reviewed in this publication in order to gain a better understanding of the level of penetration of these technologies.

At the macro level, it is possible to trace broad changes in the patterns of development and diffusion of labour-saving technologies and practices. For example, there has been a trend away from subsidized distribution of technologies such as stoves or grinding mills through development projects towards more widespread dissemination through private commercial channels. There has been a similar change in the delivery of basic services such as water and energy supplies – away from small, project-based approaches towards commercial supply of piped water and grid electricity. In general, the available evidence suggests that while commercial distribution of products, technologies and basic services can speed up the rate of diffusion of improved technologies, marginal groups such as poor rural women will tend to be excluded because of their lack of purchasing power.

At the same time, strategies involving the scaling-up of projects that focus on the inclusion of rural poor women are extremely resource-intensive and sometimes fail to reach sufficiently large numbers of people in the short to medium term. This helps to explain why millions of women in rural areas are still overburdened despite the availability of technologies that could decrease the time they spend on routine tasks and increase their productivity. Obviously,

Credit: Susan Beccio/IFAD

Land preparation in advance of potato planting is still done by hand in this village in Turkey.

there is a need to identify ways of overcoming the constraints involved in the strategies that have been used to promote technology development and diffusion.

The following section pulls together some of the lessons that can be learned from existing experiences with a view to improving future policies and programmes aimed at increasing women's access to improved technologies and their ability to benefit from these.

Lessons learned from case studies

The case studies included in this review cover a range of women's domestic, on-farm and off-farm tasks and a range of regions and countries with a focus on poorer rural women in agriculture-based economies. In total, they provide an overview of the types of interventions that various international and local agencies have introduced in the past 30 years in an attempt to release women's time and energy from non-productive domestic chores and to increase the productivity of their labour in farming and non-farm enterprises.

The findings from these case studies can be divided into two major groups:

- those that relate to the dissemination of labour-saving technologies and practices in terms of appropriateness, acceptability, fit with priority needs and accessibility; and

- those that relate to the impact of these technologies on different types of women in terms of meeting practical and strategic needs and sustainability.

Dissemination

Many of the labour-saving technologies introduced through development projects or available through commercial channels have not found widespread acceptance among rural women. There are several reasons for this, and acceptance levels could have been improved if only the relevant questions had been asked, the appropriate linkages made at the stage of technology development and the appropriate strategies implemented in disseminating useful technologies. Questions include: Is it any better? Is it acceptable? Does it meet a priority need? Is it accessible?

Is it any better?

Sometimes, as is the case with many semi-mechanized crop-processing machines, the so-called 'improved' technologies are not much more efficient than traditional technologies and so do not merit the extra investment involved. In other cases, the technologies have been imported from other countries and introduced without adaptation. Or, they have been adapted by local manufacturers and artisans without proper consultation with potential users. When, as a result, these do not meet the specific needs of the users, they tend to be rejected.

When research and development institutions, local manufacturers and artisans have been able to find a way to relate to women users and to incorporate their ideas into the design and adaptation process – as was the case with smoking ovens and cassava graters in West Africa – then improved technologies have been successfully disseminated. Ways need to be found to replicate such experiences in other developing countries, such as those in East and Southern Africa where there is much less interaction between blacksmiths who produce farm equipment and rural women who are their potential clients. In addition, as the case of *dadawwa* in Nigeria demonstrates, rural women often come up with technological adaptations of their own in response to drought, deforestation or other external changes. Examples such as this need to be identified and women's own technological capabilities and efforts supported.

Is it acceptable?

In some cases, women have rejected labour-saving technologies for socio-cultural reasons such as local taboos on working with oxen, using long-handled hoes or riding bicycles. While it is important to be sensitive to cultural issues, they can represent a major constraint on economic development. In some parts of the developing world, taboos have been overcome as a matter of necessity. Many African women are now using oxen because they have been forced to take over men's farming tasks as a result of increased rural to urban migration and the spread of HIV and AIDS. Evidence suggests that they may be subject to ridicule and pressure when they first start doing work that is traditionally men's, but that this can be successfully overcome when local agencies lend encouragement and support. A report from Ethiopia shows that innovative women have even been able to act as role models and go on to train other women to use oxen (Haile, 2004). In India, there is evidence that given sufficient time and observable benefits, communities will accept changes such as women riding bicycles. Examples like these can be used as role models for women and men in other parts of the world.

Does it meet a priority need?

There are also cases of women rejecting labour-saving technologies because these do not respond to their priority needs. Some improved stoves that save significant amounts of time in collecting firewood have been rejected because they do not meet the more pressing need of saving time in the cooking process itself. Labour-saving technologies are much more likely to gain general acceptance and result in widespread benefits if the need for them has been expressed by rural women themselves. For example, the UNDP/IFAD Multi-functional Platforms Project in West Africa has been successful, among other reasons, because it has responded to requests for the acquisition of platforms only from women's associations and is thus demand rather than supply led.

In the case of provision of basic services such as piped water and roads, these have often met the needs of men in the community rather than those of women. A major reason for this is that women tend to be excluded in the consultations held when major infrastructure programmes are being planned. Ensuring full involvement of rural women in all planning and decision-making processes, as was the case with the Peru Rural Roads Program, is the only way of ensuring that women's priority needs are met.

Is it accessible?

Even when labour-saving technologies are appropriate, culturally acceptable and meet a priority need, there are many factors that limit women's ability to benefit from them. Major constraints relate to women's lack of access to information on technologies, lack of access to cash and credit and lack of access to training and technical skills.

Access to information: As seen with farm implements in East Africa, women often do not know the range of technologies that are available. Traditional government extension services provide a narrow range of information that, in the case of agriculture, is normally restricted to seeds and fertilizers rather than tools (IFAD Technical Advisory Division, 1998). And while there is increased awareness of the need for extension workers to engage with women, and many extension services now recruit women, services still tend to be male dominated – and male extension workers tend to interact more easily with men than with women. In some countries, such as India, commercial companies make an effort to both undertake market research for agricultural tools and equipment and for household items such as improved stoves and lamps and to incorporate the views of women, whom they recognize as the ultimate consumers. In much of Africa, however, commercial companies rarely do market research or supply information to potential clients, and any sales channels or after-sales services that are available tend to be staffed by men and relate to men, thus replicating the bias of extension services. Rural women are more likely to be able to form links with local blacksmiths with mutual benefits. However, efforts are not always made to fully include local artisans in supply chains, and insufficient attention is given to strengthening linkages between women users, local producers and outside sources of information.

For a long time, reaching people living in poverty with information was characterized as the 'last mile problem', a term borrowed from the telecommunications field, where it referred to the difficulty of improving connectivity in remote rural areas. In recent years, this 'problem' has been reconceptualized as 'connecting the first mile', which privileges the needs of people living in those remote areas (Talyarkhan et al., 2005). One of the projects that has adopted this approach is IFAD's First Mile Project, which is being implemented in collaboration with the Agricultural Marketing Systems Development Programme of the Government of Tanzania (IFAD, 2006b). The project assists small farmers, traders, processors and others from poor rural areas to build market chains linking producers to consumers. People in isolated rural communities use mobile phones, e-mail and even the Internet to share their local experiences and good practices, learning from each other.

An example of what the project has been able to achieve comes from five farmers' associations that – through the use of mobile phones, price updates broadcast by radio and market intelligence collected by *shushushus,* or market spies – were able to sell maize at more than double the price obtained by other farmers' groups who did not have access to near real-time market intelligence. Overall, in the first 10 months of implementation, the project, with an initial investment of $200,000, was estimated to have contributed to an increase in income of participants of more than $1.8 million (IFAD, 2007a). Building on this experience, IFAD has provided a grant of $1.5 million to FAO over three years to support a Rural Knowledge Network project for East Africa that will work with farmers and their organizations to build a region-wide knowledge management process that responds to farmers' demands and generates and delivers information to meet their particular requirements in a useful form.

However, while many such projects have successfully promoted the use of new ICTs to get information to women and men farmers about market prices, they have not gone the extra mile in terms of using these as a way of supplying information about the range of labour-saving technologies that are available. Some non-governmental initiatives are moving ahead in trying to fill this information gap. One example is the vast network of village kiosks and coordinating hubs that has been set up by the M.S. Swaminathan Research Foundation (MSSRF) in India to link rural women virtually with scientists and technologists who can respond to their problems and requests for information. Swaminathan set up the first of his telecom kiosks in the late 1990s and there are now 80 kiosks across 3 states. These have been used successfully by farmers, with the help of trained volunteers, to track down solutions to problems with food production and processing. The hope is that ICTs will provide a fresh approach to agricultural extension, putting the information directly in the farmers' hands. Eventually, the aim is to have 100,000 kiosks – one for every 6 of India's 600,000 villages (Fairless, 2007).

Another example is the Women of Uganda Network project on 'Enhancing Access to Agricultural Information Using Information and Communication Technologies in Apac District'. In collaboration with government programmes, this seeks to use mobile phones, radio cassettes, community radio and the Internet to bridge the gap between researchers, extension workers and women farmers. The project is based on the results of a study undertaken in 2003, which found that rural farmers lacked information on sources of inputs/implements as well as other constraints including how to improve seeds and crop varieties and improve skills (Women of Uganda Network, n.d.).

Access to cash and credit: Another major barrier to women's access to labour-saving technologies is their lack of access to cash and a reluctance on the part of their husbands to contribute towards such technologies when they feel that the work can be done (as it always has been) free of charge by women. As long as women's labour is perceived as having little or no value, then limited progress can be expected. However, experience shows that three strategies can be effective. First, research findings that put an economic value on women's time spent on survival tasks can be more widely disseminated to decision makers and rural communities as a tool for advocating for the introduction of labour-saving technologies on economic grounds.

Second, strategies can be introduced that increase the chances of the time saved by women being redeployed in economically productive ways so that they are better able to cover the costs of labour-saving devices. This was the case with the IFAD biogas project in China, which provided loans for women's income-generating activities as an integral part of the project (IFAD, 2007b). A particularly successful strategy is that used in projects including stoves in Kenya, lamps in Peru and energy services in Mali, which stimulate income directly through engaging local women in the manufacturing and selling of energy technologies, as well as indirectly through gains in productivity or expanded economic activity resulting from new energy inputs.

Third, and perhaps most controversial, is the strategy of increasing women's access to credit so that they can afford to buy labour-saving technologies – either individually or in groups. Microfinance has been put forward as the new 'silver bullet' for alleviating poverty, and one of its major selling points is its alleged ability to empower women. Certainly, microfinance has attracted untold billions of dollars, but its impact on women in general – and its ability to assist them to purchase labour-saving technologies in particular – is increasingly questioned. According to one recent study 'micro-loans are more beneficial to borrowers living above the poverty line.... This is because clients with more income are willing to take the risks, such as investing in technologies, that will most likely increase income flows. Poor borrowers, on the other hand, tend to take out conservative loans that protect their subsistence, and rarely invest in new technology' (Karnani, 2007).

Another problem with microfinance is that the amounts available to women are simply not sufficient for acquiring labour-saving or productivity-increasing technologies. As a result, women are trapped in low-income endeavours and lack the means to increase the amount of cash they have to invest in technological improvements that would improve their lives and livelihoods. For example, a recent study of rural energy projects found that micro-loans were not of sufficient size to help women to acquire energy equipment (Karlsson and McDade, 2001). A common strategy has been to form women into groups for the purpose of dispensing loans, but group activities have proved less than successful in some cultures and, in general, technologies owned and operated by individuals have spread more quickly and worked more efficiently than those owned by groups – although not always with equitable distribution of benefits.

Access to training and technical skills: Lack of access to training and skills has also proved to be a barrier to women's use of technologies since it is often men rather than women who are targeted for training opportunities. When women are given the chance to learn new skills, as with the female barefoot solar engineers in India and women solar technicians in Uganda, they show that they are well able to put this to good use. Similarly, women volunteer workers trained at the National Virtual Academy established by the MSSRF in India have proved to be very successful at helping women and men farmers solve problems by linking them to researchers through village telecom kiosks.

Experience also shows that women are extremely good at sharing new knowledge with each other. This happened with adaptations to traditional production of *daddawa* in Nigeria, for example, where the technology of soybean growing and processing has been spread from women to women by word of mouth, without any formal groupings, structures or procedures. Peer training and exchange of experience can often be more effective tools in spreading improved technologies and techniques than formal training courses.

Impact

Reaching women with labour-saving technologies is only half of the battle. Experience shows that outcomes are not always as expected and that short-term practical benefits can sometimes be lost if the use of the technologies does not lead to longer-term strategic changes.

Difficulties in measuring impact

Measuring impact is a difficult task. While it is easy to put a figure on the amount of time that women can save through using a particular technology, it is much more difficult to trace how women make use of this time. Sometimes, it is simply used to collect more water or fuel wood or to farm more land than was possible before, or to reduce the amount of time that children must spend on such activities. Sometimes, it is used to earn more income. And sometimes, it is put into social and community activities such as visiting friends and family or attending literacy classes and committee meetings. Often, it is split between all such uses.

Several recent studies have commented on the need for improved methods of measuring the impact of labour-saving technologies to provide data that would be instrumental in informing government policies and programmes that determine their development and diffusion. For example, the recent FAO study on gender and energy states that 'energy programmes should evaluate the impacts of their initiatives on women and men. For this purpose, they should use indicators that are gender-disaggregated and be able to record improvements in women's position and negative impacts on women's conditions, in terms of convenience, quality of life and access to and control over resources. However, these indicators are generally more qualitative than quantitative. Furthermore, they are also harder to measure'. As a result it recommends the further development of indicators by the international community of agencies including FAO and IFAD (Lambrou and Piana, 2006).

Differential impact

While increasing attention is given to the differential impact of technical change on women and men, much less has been focused on the differential impact on different categories of women – women in different regions and from different types and levels of household status. As we have seen, women in poor and landless households living in areas of labour surplus such as Asia are more likely to be displaced than helped by labour-saving on-farm technologies. In these circumstances, more schemes such as those introduced by BRAC in Bangladesh are needed if the poorest women are to share more equally in the benefits associated with modern farm machinery.

Access versus control

In assessing the impact of improved technologies on women and men, there is often a tendency to look only at access rather than at ownership and control. But, as was seen with farming implements in Africa and bicycles in India, when women have access to a technology rather than control over how and when it can be used, the potential benefits are significantly reduced. This issue relates directly to the distinction between meeting women's practical and strategic needs. While many projects result in practical benefits for rural women, such as greater availability of water or fuel wood, there are fewer projects that meet strategic needs in terms of changing the balance of power within the household or increasing women's ability to negotiate effectively with local decision makers.

Attempts have been made to promote cooperative ownership with mixed results. However, experience shows that when the need and the benefits are great enough, as with the case of the women's bus cooperative in Kenya, women can take control of their own lives through ownership of modern technology. In addition, women's associations, such as those that own and operate multi-functional platforms in West Africa, have proved to be more successful than older-style women's groups and cooperatives.

The strategies used to introduce new technologies can in themselves have an influence on women's ability to play a role in decision-making and thus determine results. For example, community-based infrastructure projects lend themselves much more to women's empowerment than large-scale top-down government programmes. And technologies that lead to an increase in women's earning capacity are much more likely to increase women's status and decision-making powers within the household and community – thus strengthening the argument for labour-saving technologies that release women's time to engage in income-generating activities.

Unexpected outcomes

Experience shows that the introduction of labour-saving technologies can have some unexpected results. For example, it can lead to changes in the division of labour within the household, and it can also lead to men taking over women's traditional industries when these become more profitable. To the extent such changes deprive women of income-earning opportunities, they need to be addressed through measures that support women's ownership and control of the technologies involved. Ideally, the potential for such outcomes should be assessed during the appraisal of proposed interventions. In addition, short-term gains that women derive from some labour-saving technologies can be lost if there is no system in place to maintain and repair them. Training women to undertake such tasks can serve the double purpose of keeping systems in operation and providing a useful source of income.

External forces

Finally, national and international policy and regulations can and do have a major influence on the way in which technologies are developed/acquired and diffused, and on the way in which costs and benefits are distributed.

In general, trade liberalization policies have encouraged the import of agricultural tools and agro-processing machines that are less suited to local needs in many cases than those produced by local artisans and offer fewer opportunities for linkages between producers and users. Privatization of water and electricity services has often improved supplies for richer segments of the population at the expense of the poor majority living in rural areas, who are deprived of support for community-based infrastructure projects. And lack of investment of the public sector in research and development and in training and extension facilities has resulted in much of the work on technology development and diffusion being left in the hands of the private sector, which has tended to exclude the rural poor (and especially women) who have no access to cash or credit.

However, there seems to be some light at the end of the tunnel, with a number of success stories where governments and international agencies have made the effort to support the development and diffusion of basic needs technologies to poor rural women and men. These include micro-hydro plants in Nepal and multi-functional platforms in Mali that promote development through the supply of electricity on a decentralized basis. Although women have benefited from time savings in both cases, they have not always had an equal share with men in decision-making or equal ownership opportunities. Additional policies and support measures, such as quotas for women's participation in management committees or affirmative action in dispersal of grants and loans, are needed to ensure gender equity. Donor agencies have played a major role in promoting ownership of multi-functional platforms by women's associations in Mali, and the Government of Nepal is promoting participation of women in management committees dealing with irrigation and forest resources, as well as micro-hydro systems. While there is still some need for improvement, policies and programmes such as these need to be better documented with a view to widespread replication.

CHAPTER 5
Where do we go from here?

IN MOVING FORWARD on increasing the access of rural women to the labour-saving technologies and practices that they need to contribute to and benefit fully from economic development, we need to consider two major issues:

- what needs to be done to overcome constraints that have limited the diffusion of technologies that already exist; and
- how lessons can be learned from past experience when developing and diffusing 'new' technologies that aim to address women's time and energy poverty.

Existing technologies and practices

Although many labour-saving technologies and practices exist that could assist women with their domestic chores and in their farming and non-farm activities, these have failed to be diffused and used successfully on anything like the scale required. A major problem in tackling this is the lack of detailed statistics on the numbers of such technologies and practices being used by women and men in different types of households in different countries, and there is an obvious need to improve data collection in this respect.

Another problem has been the failure to learn from micro-level experiences and, on the basis of this experience, to adopt strategies that can contribute to the widespread diffusion of successfully tested technologies. Some important measures have been identified that could help to overcome constraints. These include:

Integrated packages. Different aspects of women's work and lives are so intertwined that it makes little sense to try to deal with any one aspect in isolation. Thus, rural transport projects should not be dealt with separately from water supply, rural energy supply and health provision projects. Similarly, it needs to be recognized that water and energy have multiple uses, and projects should be designed to take both multi-use and multi-user realities into consideration. Further, programmes that incorporate measures to reduce the time women spend in subsistence activities should have components that facilitate their increased involvement in income-generating activities.

Capacity building. Attention has to be paid to women's strategic needs in terms of empowerment as well as their practical needs in terms of increased access to water, energy and transport. To this end, it is important to provide for women's involvement in the planning and implementation of community-level schemes and to ensure they are fully represented in meetings convened with communities prior to the implementation of large-scale infrastructure projects.

Linking local researchers, producers and users. Technologies are unlikely to respond to women's priorities and needs unless women have been involved in the design process. Accordingly, programmes and projects should reduce their emphasis on imported technologies and support local blacksmiths and artisans instead. This will make it more likely that women's voices will be heard in the design and adaptation process and better ensure that tools and equipment can be maintained and repaired in a timely and cost-effective manner. ICTs can play an important role in building linkages between research and development institutions and women users; and linkages can be promoted between researchers and the local artisans who are best placed to bring about the commercialization of technologies needed by rural women.

Supporting the losers from technical change. When the introduction of a labour-saving technology means that one group of women can only be helped at the expense of another, then measures need to be incorporated in projects to ensure that the losers are assisted to diversify into alternative ways of making an income. This can involve various organizing strategies and provision of credit, skills training and information on new economic opportunities including those that involve the production, maintenance and repair of labour-saving technologies.

In general, however, the major reason why existing technologies have been unable to reach and bring benefits to a large number of rural women is the failure to find appropriate strategies that address the underlying sources of rural poverty and gender inequality. While commercialization of technologies and basic service provision through the private sector seems to be the most efficient way of reaching more people, marginal and vulnerable groups – and especially rural women – tend to be excluded because of their lack of knowledge and access to cash with which to buy these products or services. At the same time, strategies aiming to scale-up pilot projects that have taken women's cash and time constraints into consideration are extremely resource-intensive and result in a much slower, albeit more equitable, rate of diffusion. The challenge for the future is to find some combination of these two strategies that brings to bear the best properties of each.

Two recent initiatives, if successful, promise to bring about a significant increase in the number of 'existing' technologies available to rural women. One of these is the joint venture by the Shell Foundation and Envirofit to produce and market millions of improved wood-burning stoves, and the other is the initiative of UNDP and the Gates Foundation to increase the use of multi-functional platforms in Africa. By combining significant amounts of financial support with strategies designed to include many of the lessons learned from past successes and failures, initiatives such as these may well stand a chance of at last bringing about a sea-change in the way in which gender and technology issues are tackled. This is especially so given the recent recognition of the fact that the 4 billion people who live in relative poverty have a purchasing power representing $5 trillion, and an increased focus by international agencies on helping companies to think more creatively about new business models that meet the needs of this huge and largely unmet market (International Financial Corporation/World Resources Institute, 2008).

Some 25 years ago, one of the more prominent researchers on appropriate technology suggested that an 'AT General Electric' was needed that would market millions of village stoves (Jequier, 1983). It is possible that the renewed interest in saving women's time in tasks such as fuel wood collection, which has emerged from external trends such as the spread of HIV and AIDS and rapid climate change, may provide the ideal environment for this 'wish' to become a reality.

New technologies

As noted earlier, policy interest has turned in recent years to the potential of the so-called 'new' technologies – ICTs, biotechnology, biofuels and nanotechnology – in helping to solve problems of food insecurity, lack of access to safe drinking water and high rates of deaths due to malnutrition and diseases such as malaria, tuberculosis and AIDS. As such, they could offer ways to reduce the time women spend on collecting water and fuel wood and taking care of the sick while at the same time improving their health and productivity. However, there is growing concern that the funding being directed towards the development and diffusion of these technologies may not be pro-poor. There are four major reasons for this.

First, there is evidence that research and development on new technologies is being geared towards the wants of richer consumers rather than the needs of the poor and, that a 'digital divide' and a 'nano divide' are emerging and increasing in size. Data already reveal that 90 per cent of all medical research is targeted at problems affecting only 10 per cent of the world's population. Similarly, many new seed varieties are engineered to be suitable for mechanized mass-production designed for industrial and intensive-farming conditions, while very little attention has been given to the needs of small farmers in developing countries in terms of developing biotechnologies that increase the nutritional value or drought resistance of crops (Chataway, 2005; UNDP, 1999).

Second, even if a new technology addresses a priority need of the rural poor, it may not be the best or most appropriate way of doing so. For example, evidence is emerging that improved traditional or existing technologies can solve the problem of filtering out impurities in drinking water at a lower cost and in a more appropriate way than can nanotechnology; and, while there is undoubtedly a role for newly engineered seeds designed to provide added vitamins in some parts of the developing world, many researchers claim that indigenous crops such as *quinoa* contain as many nutrients and have fewer negative side effects (Grimshaw, 2007; Shiva, 2000).

Third, some new technologies such as biofuels may solve one problem (such as time spent on fuel wood collection or health problems caused by indoor pollution) at the risk of creating others (such as shortages or increased prices of food) that have a negative impact on women's lives and livelihoods. And fourth, even when a new technology could address the needs of rural women, the infrastructure to make it operational – such as electricity, agricultural extension services or public health systems – is simply not available.

In conclusion, if lessons are not learned from the past 30 years of experience in the development and diffusion of labour-saving technologies and practices, then development planners and practitioners and scientists and technologists are in danger of making all of the same mistakes again. It is hoped that this review of experiences will add to a better understanding of the strategies that could and should be adopted in the future.

References

Adjebeng-Asem, S. (1990) 'The Nigerian cassava grater', in Gamser, M. et al. (eds), *Tinker, Tiller, Technical Change,* IT Publications, London.

Ahmad, M. and Jenkins, A. (1989) 'Traditional paddy husking: an appropriate technology under pressure', in Carr, M. (ed.), *Women and the Food Cycle,* IT Publications, London.

Appleton, H. (1994) 'Technological innovation in women's microenterprises', *Small Enterprise Development,* 5(1).

Atukorala, K. and Amerasekera, R.M. (2006) 'Case study of scaled-up improved cookstove: The Practical Action Project', Practical Action South Asia, Colombo.

Barwell, I. and Calvo, C.M. (1989) *Makete Integrated Rural Transport Project – The Transport Demands of Rural Households: Findings from a village-level travel survey,* Volume 1: Main Report, ILO, Geneva.

Bates, L. (ed.) (2007) *Smoke, Health and Household Energy,* Volume 2, Practical Action, Bourton on Dunsmore.

Bhattarai, H.P. et al. (2006) *Status of Governance in Community Managed Micro-Hydropower Plants in Nepal,* Practical Action, Bourton on Dunsmore.

Bishop-Sambrook, C. (2003) 'Labour-saving technologies and practices for farming and household activities in Eastern and Southern Africa', joint study by IFAD/FAO, Rome.

Bishop-Sambrook, C., Kienzle, J., Mariki, W., Owenya, M. and Ribeiro F. (2004) 'Conservation Agriculture as a labour saving practice for vulnerable households: A study of the suitability of reduced tillage and cover crops for households under labour stress in Babati and Karatu Districts, Northern Tanzania', joint study by IFAD/FAO, Rome.

Blackden, C.M. and Wodon, Q. (2006) 'Gender, time use and poverty: Introduction' in Blackden, C.M. and Wodon, Q. (eds), *Gender, Time Use and Poverty in Sub-Saharan Africa,* World Bank Working Paper #17, World Bank, Washington, DC.

Burn, N. and Coche, L. (2001) 'Multifunctional platform for village power', in Misana, S. and Karlsson, G.V. (eds), *Generating Opportunities: Case studies on energy and women,* UNDP, New York.

Carr, M. (ed.) (1989) *Women and the Food Cycle,* IT Publications, London.

Carr, M. and Chen, M. (2004) 'Globalization, social exclusion and gender', *International Labour Review,* 143(1/2).

Carr, M. and Marjoram, T. (forthcoming) *Minding the Gap: Technology, policy and poverty reduction,* UNESCO and Practical Action Publishing, Paris/Bourton on Dunsmore.

Carr, M. and Sandhu, R. (1987) 'Women, technology and rural productivity', *UNIFEM Occasional Paper #6,* UNIFEM, New York.

Cecelski, E. (1984) *The Rural Energy Crisis, Women's Work and Family Welfare: Perspectives and approaches to action,* ILO, Geneva.

Cecelski, E. (2004) 'Re-thinking gender and energy: old and new directions', ENERGIA/Enabling Access to Sustainable Energy (EASE) Discussion Paper, ETC International, Leusden.

Chataway, J. (2005) 'Introduction: Is it possible to create pro-poor agriculture-related biotechnology', *Journal of International Development*, 17(5).

Chaudhuri, S. (2007) 'The gap between successful innovation and access to its benefits: Indian pharmaceuticals', *European Journal of Development Research*, 19(1), March.

Clancy, J.S. and Kooijman, A. (2006) 'Enabling access to sustainable energy: A synthesis of research findings in Bolivia, Tanzania and Vietnam', research report, Department for Technology and Sustainable Development, University of Twente.

Dianzheng, L. (2007) 'Bringing natural light to remote households in China', *Making a Difference in Asia and the Pacific*, Issue 15, March/April [online] www.ifad.org/newsletter/pi/15.htm [Accessed 5 June 2009].

Fairless, D. (2007) 'From wheat to web: Children of the revolution', *Nature*, 449(7165): 964–966.

Fernando, P. and Porter, G. (2002) 'Introduction' in Fernando, P. and Porter, G. (eds), *Balancing the Load: Women, gender and transport*, Zed Books, London.

Ghertner, D.A. (2006) 'Technology and tricks: Intra-household technology improvements and gender studies', *Gender, Technology and Development*, 10(3).

Gender and Rural Transport Initiative (GRTI) (2006a) 'Donkey Project in Uganda', *GRTI Country Report #14*, World Bank, Washington, DC.

GRTI (2006b) 'Using a cart for water supplies in Kaolack', *GRTI Country Report #11*, World Bank, Washington, DC.

Grimshaw, D.J. (2007) 'Nano-dialogues: Helping scientists to meet poor people's needs', *ID21 Insights*, 68.

Gupta, S. (2007) 'Barefoot, female and a solar engineer', *India Together*, 19 October.

Haggblade, S., Reardon, T. and Hyman, E. (2007) 'Technology as a Motor of Change in the Rural Nonfarm Economy', in Haggblade, S., Hazell, P.B.R. and Reardon, T. (eds), *Transforming the Rural Nonfarm Economy: Opportunities and threats in the developing world*, World Bank and IFPRI, Washington, DC.

Haile, M. (2004) 'Ethiopia: A woman innovator speaks', *IK Notes*, no. 70, July.

Helps International (n.d.) 'The ONIL Stove', [online] www.helpsinternational.com/programs/stove.php [Accessed 5 June 2009].

Huyer, S., Hafkin, N., Ertl, D. and Dryburgh, H. (2005) 'Women in the Information Society', in Sciadis, G. (ed.), *From Digital Divide to Digital Opportunities: Measuring infostates for development*, Orbicom, Montreal.

Hyman, E. (1993) 'Production of edible oils for the masses and by the masses: The impact of the ram press in Tanzania', *World Development*, 21(3): 429–443.

International Fund for Agricultural Development (IFAD) (2006a), 'Central Dry Area Small Holder and Community Services Development Project (CKDAP), Kenya', Supervision Mission Report, Rome.

IFAD (2006b) 'Bringing markets closer in the United Republic of Tanzania', [online], *Update*, Issue 2, February, www.ifad.org/newsletter/update/2/6.htm [Accessed 5 June 2009].

IFAD (2007a) 'Rural Women's Walking Time', [online], Rural Poverty Portal, January, www.ifad.org/ [Accessed 5 June 2009].

IFAD (2007b) 'Wulin Mountains Minority-Areas Development Project, China, Supervision Mission Report: Crosscutting Issues', project report, May, IFAD, Rome.

IFAD Technical Advisory Division (1998) *Agricultural Implements Used by Women Farmers in Africa*, IFAD/Japan Overseas Development Assistance/ FAO, Rome.

International Financial Corporation/World Resources Institute (2008) *The Next 4 Billion: Market size and business strategy at the base of the pyramid*, World Bank, Washington, DC.

Ilkarraccan I. and Appleton, H. (1995) *Women's Roles in Technical Innovation*, UNIFEM Food Cycle Technology Source Books, UNIFEM, New York.

International Labour Organization/Netherlands Government (1985) *Field Report on Post-Adoption Studies: Technologies for rural women*, ILO, Geneva.

Intermediate Technology Development Group (1986) 'Internal Report on Nepal', ITDG, Rugby.

International Telecommunications Union (ITU) (2007) 'Key Global Telecom Indicators for the World Telecommunications Service Sector', [online], ITU, Geneva, www.itu.int/ITU-D/ict/statistics/at_glance/KeyTelecom99. hmtl [Accessed 5 June 2009].

Jequier, N. (1983) 'Small is beautiful – and becoming big', *Appropriate Technology*, 10(3), December.

Karlsson, G.V. and McDade, S. (2001) 'Introduction' in Misana, S. and Karlsson, G.V. (eds), *Generating Opportunities: Case studies on energy and women*, UNDP, New York.

Karnani, A. (2007) 'Microfinance misses its mark', *Stanford Social Innovation Review*, Summer.

Kneerim, J. (1980) *Village Women Organize: The Mraru bus service*, SEEDS, New York.

Lambrou Y. and Piana, G. (2006) *Energy and Gender Issues in Rural Sustainable Development*, FAO, Rome.

Maguzu, C.W. et al. (2007) 'Arumeru District' in Shetto, R. and Owenya, M.(eds), *Conservation Agriculture as Practised in Tanzania: Three case studies*, African Conservation Tillage Network, Nairobi.

Matuschke, I. (2007) 'Case Study: Conservation Agriculture in Tanzania', internal document, IFAD, Rome.

McCall, M. (2001) 'Brewing rural beer should be a hotter issue', *Boiling Point*, Issue 47.

McCann, B. (1998) *Building Bridges: A review of infrastructure services projects addressing gender integration*, CIDA, Hull, Quebec.

Mehta, L. and Madsen, B.L. (2005) 'Is the WTO after your water? The General Agreement on Trade and Services (GATS) and poor people's right to water', *Natural Resources Forum*, 29(2): 154–164.

Mensah, S.A. (2001) 'Energy for rural women's enterprises' in Misana, S. and Karlsson, G.V. (eds), *Generating Opportunities: Case studies on energy and women*, UNDP, New York.

Misana, S. and Karlsson, G.V. (eds), *Generating Opportunities: Case studies on energy and women*, UNDP, New York.

Mwankusye, J. (2002) 'Do intermediate means of transport reach rural women?' in Fernando, P. and Porter, G. (eds), *Balancing the Load: Women, Gender and transport*, Zed Books, London.

Njenga, B.K. (2001) 'Upesi Rural Stoves Project' in Misana, S. and Karlsson, G.V. (eds), *Generating Opportunities: Case studies on energy and women*, UNDP, New York.

Owala, H.N. (2001) 'The development and marketing of Upesi stoves: A case study of successful women from west Kenya', *Boiling Point*, Issue 47.

Paris, T. and Chi, T.T.N. (2005) 'The impact of row seeder technology on women labor: A case study of the Mekong Delta, Vietnam', *Gender, Technology and Development*, 9(2): 157–184.

Peters, D. (2001) 'Gender and transport in less developed countries: A background paper in preparation for CSD9', paper commissioned by the UNED Forum for the Expert Workshop on Gender Perspectives for Earth Summit 2002, Berlin, 10–12 January.

Practical Action (2008) 'Liquid biofuels to alleviate poverty', *Technical Brief #5*, Practical Action, Bourton on Dunsmore.

Rao, N. (2002) 'Cycling into the future: The Pudukkottai experience' Fernando, P. and Porter, G. (eds), *Balancing the Load: Women, Gender and transport*, Zed Books, London.

Raswant, V., Hart, N. and Romano, M. (2008) 'Biofuel expansion: Challenges, risks and opportunities for rural poor people', paper prepared for the Round Table organized during the Thirty-first Session of IFAD's Governing Council, 14 February.

Redhouse, D. (2005) *Getting to Boiling Point: Turning up the heat on water and sanitation*, WaterAid, London.

Rossi, A. and Lambrou, Y. (2008) *Gender and Equity Issues in Liquid Biofuels Production: Minimizing the risks to maximize the opportunities*, FAO, Rome.

Sandhu, R. (1989) 'Women and fish smoking', in M. Carr (ed.), *Women and the Food Cycle*, IT Publications, London.

Scott, P.L. (2005) 'Rocket stoves for Sub-Saharan Africa', *Boiling Point*, Issue 50.

Sengendo, M.C. (2001) 'Photovoltaic project for rural electrification', in Misana, S. and Karlsson, G.V. (eds), *Generating Opportunities: Case studies on energy and women*, UNDP, New York.

Shaffer, R. (2007) 'Unplanned obsolescence', *Fast Company Magazine* #118, [on-line], www.fastcompany.com/magazine/118/unplanned-obsolescence. html [Accessed 5 June 2009].

Shiva, V. (2000) *Stolen Harvest*, South End Press, Cambridge, MA.

Spence, N. (1986) *Impact of Technology on Women in Crop Processing*, CIDA, Hull, Quebec.

Stokes, H. and Ebbeson, B. (2005) 'Project Gaia: Commercializing a new stove and new fuel in Africa', *Boiling Point*, Issue 50.

Talyarkhan, S., Grimshaw, D.J. and Lowe, L. (2005) 'Connecting the first mile: A best practice framework for ICT-based knowledge sharing initiatives', in Rahman, H. (ed.), *Empowering Marginal Communities with Information Networking*, IDEA Books, Harrisburg, PA.

Tanzarn, N. (2003) *Integrating Gender into World Bank Financed Transport Programmes. Case Study, Uganda, Road Sector Programme Support (RSPS)*, World Bank, Washington, DC.

Thomas, S., Rajepakse, I.R. and Gunasekara, J. (2007) 'Turning off the lights: GATS and the threat to community electricity in Sri Lanka', [online], *ITDG Practical Answers to Poverty*, http://practicalaction.org/docs/advocacy/gats_and_electricity_in_sri_lanka.pdf [Accessed 5 June 2009].

United Nations Development Programme (UNDP) (1995) *Human Development Report 1995: Gender and Human Development*, Oxford University Press, New York.

UNDP (1999) *Human Development Report 1999: Globalization with a human face*, Oxford University Press, New York.

UNDP (2006) *Human Development Report 2006: Beyond scarcity: Power, poverty and the global water crisis*, Oxford University Press, New York.

UNDP (2008) 'The Gates Foundation grants US$19 million to women's programs in West Africa', Newsroom, [online], 22 February, http://content.undp.org/go/newsroom/2008/february/gates-foundation-grants-west-african-women.en [Accessed 5 June 2009].

United Nations Statistical Division (UNSD) (1995) *The World's Women 1995: Trends and statistics 1970–1990*, United Nations, New York.

UNSD (2000) *The World's Women 2000: Trends and statistics*, United Nations, New York.

UNSD (2005) *The World's Women 2005: Progress in statistics*, United Nations, New York.

Utthan Development Action Planning Team (2001) 'Women, water and community ownership', *India Together*, January [online] www.indiatogether.org/stories/utthan.htm [Accessed 5 June 2009].

Venter, C. and Mashiri, M. (2007) *Gender and Transport: Towards a practical analysis framework for improved planning*, University of Pretoria.

von Braun, J. (2007) *The World Food Situation: New driving forces and required actions*, IFPRI, Washington, DC.

Walubengo, D. (1995) 'No money, no stoves', in Westhoff, B. and Germann, D. (eds), *Stove Images: A documentation of improved and traditional stoves in Africa, Asia and Latin America*, Brandes & Apsel Verlag GmbH, Frankfurt.

Wahaj, R. (2007) *Gender and Water: Securing water for improved rural livelihoods: The multiple uses systems approach*, IFAD, Rome.

Wahaj, R. and Hartl, M. (2007) 'Women continue to be excluded from water user associations', *Making a Difference in Asia and the Pacific*, Issue 17, September/October.

Wang, H. (2007) 'Maintaining and managing biogas tanks through local associations', *Making a Difference in Asia and the Pacific*, Issue 15, March/April.

Women of Uganda Network (n.d.) 'Access 4Dev Projects', [online], www.wougnet.org [Accessed 25 August 2008].

World Bank (2004) 'Making rural roads work for both women and men: The example of Peru's Rural Roads Program', [online], *Promising Approaches to Engendering Development*, http://siteresources.worldbank.org/INTGENDER/Resources/PeruRRPFINAL.pdf [Accessed 5 June 2009].

World Bank (2006) 'Gender and rural transport initiative', Module 4 in *Gender and Transport Resource Guide*, World Bank, Washington, DC.

World Bank (2008a) *World Development Report: Agriculture for development*, World Bank, Washington, DC.

World Bank (2008b) *Global Economic Prospects: Technology diffusion in developing countries*, World Bank, Washington, DC.

World Bank, FAO and IFAD (2008) *Gender in Agriculture Sourcebook*, Washington, DC.

Useful links

Many of the publications referred to in this booklet can be downloaded from these websites.

African Conservation Tillage Network: www.act.org.zw
Bill & Melinda Gates Foundation: www.gatesfoundation.org
Boiling Point: www.hedon.info
Energy Sector Management Assistance Programme: www.esmap.org
Energy and Gender Network: www.energia.org
Food and Agriculture Organization: www.fao.org
Institute of Development Studies: www.ids.ac.uk
International Food Policy Research Institute: www.ifpri.org
International Forum for Rural Transport and Development: www.ifrtd.org
International Fund for Agricultural Development: www.ifad.org
International Telecommunications Union: www.itu.int/net/home/index.aspx
Practical Action (formerly ITDG): www.practicalaction.org
Practical Action Publications (formerly IT Publications):
    www.practicalactionpublishing.org
Shell Foundation: www.shellfoundation.org
United Nations Development Programme: www.undp.org
Water Aid: www.wateraid.org/uk
Women of Uganda Network: www.wougnet.org
Women, Knowledge, Technology (WIGSAT): www.wigsat.org
World Bank: www.worldbank.org

Index